MODERN ECUMENICAL DOCUMENTS
ON THE MINISTRY

A

MODERN ECUMENICAL DOCUMENTS ON THE MINISTRY

Theodore Lownik Library
Illinois Benedictine College
Lisle, Illinois 60532

LONDON SPCK 1975

*First published in 1975
by SPCK
Holy Trinity Church
Marylebone Road
London NW1 4DU*

*Printed in Great Britain by
Church Army Press, Oxford*

SBN 281 02817 6

CONTENTS

Foreword, by the Right Reverend Alan C. Clark   vii
Joint Chairman of the Anglican–Roman Catholic
International Commission

Introduction: Modern Ecumenical Documents on   3
the Ministry, by the Right Reverend H. R. McAdoo
Joint Chairman of the Anglican–Roman Catholic
International Commission

Ministry and Ordination   29
A Statement on the Doctrine of the Ministry
Agreed by the Anglican–Roman Catholic International
Commission
Canterbury 1973

Eucharist and Ministry   53
A Lutheran–Roman Catholic Statement
St Louis, Missouri 1970

Group of Les Dombes   89
Towards a Reconciliation of Ministries
Translated by Pamela Gaughan
Les Dombes 1973

The Ordained Ministry in Ecumenical Perspective   109
An agreed statement of the Commission on Faith
and Order of the World Council of Churches
Accra, 1974

FOREWORD

The publication of *Modern Eucharistic Agreement* brought home to many the surprising convergence which had been achieved by disparate groups on the nature and significance of the eucharist. With the present publication there will be a growth in the optimism that can be detected among those charged with achieving doctrinal consensus between churches apparently separated by opposing views on the nature of the ministry. Anyone with a sense of history—and not too distant a history at that—may be excused if they are suspicious at any claim to consensus. Yet careful reading of the four documents which comprise this slim volume will show, whether the style be diffuse or concise, that there is a remarkable similarity in the way the authors of these documents have pursued their studies and in the conclusions they have reached.

In every Christian church there is an abiding conviction that it is Christ, the Lord of the Church, who directs and governs it, but uses the ministry of *men* to achieve his purpose. Within that conviction is the belief that Christ chooses from the Christian community those who are to exercise 'the ordained ministry'. At the same time the awareness that Christianity is an historical religion, deriving from the infant apostolic community which gathered together in the days after the resurrection, puts a stringent demand on every Christian church to demonstrate its own continuity with these apostolic origins. In fact, those who engage in ecumenical dialogue on the nature of ministry, find themselves forced, whatever the limitations within which they decide to concentrate their work, to face identical questions. Is the church they represent apostolic? Is the ordained ministry within that church in continuity with the church of the apostles? Does the ordained minister speak in the name of Christ and in the name of the community? Is that setting apart for the ministry, which is generally called 'ordination', something irreversible? Is apostolicity of doctrine of greater significance than continuity in ministerial office? Can one be had without the other? The questions can be multiplied, but they will always be subsumed under these or similar headings.

In the following pages the results of four ecumenical dialogues are set forth. It is for the critic to decide on their relative worth, but the ordinary reader is greatly helped by the overall analysis provided by the Bishop of Ossory in his introductory essay. These dialogues have been forced upon the Christian churches precisely because they have achieved a degree of consensus on the doctrine of the eucharist, for no eucharistic doctrine can be complete that is not integrated with a complementary doctrine of ministry.

One of the greatest theological successes of recent years has been the unanimity with which all theologians set the doctrine of the ordained ministry within the context of the ministry of the whole Church of Christ. It is no longer viewed as being in some way self-explanatory. It can, in fact, only be understood as a ministry in service to the Church, and within the Church, to enable it to exercise its common priesthood. Some of the protagonists wish to make a practical deduction from the consensus achieved, and to suggest that now the way is open to a mutual recognition of ministries (which many ecumenists regard as a high priority). Others are more reticent on the grounds that the recognition of ministries is too closely related to the recognition and reconciliation of churches to be an isolated issue. But whatever the conclusions, the Christian churches are here presented with a remarkable convergence of views and must accept the challenge this represents. The individual reader, even if all is not clear, cannot fail to be encouraged by what is clearly a very significant step in the hard road to Christian unity. Work for Christian unity is indeed highly complex, but it would collapse completely if there were not those ready to use every human resource available to construct the sort of doctrinal agreements contained in this booklet. They merit our gratitude, and once again one would like to thank Mrs Pamela Gaughan for her translation of the Dombes Agreement.

Norwich 1974

ALAN C. CLARK
Bishop of Elmham

INTRODUCTION
Modern Ecumenical Documents on the Ministry

H. R. McAdoo

© H. R. McAdoo, 1974

INTRODUCTION

Any introduction to a set of documents as potentially creative of results for the separated churches as these are, needs to clarify at the outset the nature of the material being studied.

THE QUESTION OF STATUS AND AUTHORITY

There is therefore raised at once the question of the status of the individual agreements, which varies in a number of ways, although the documents have this in common that none of them constitutes an actual inter-Church concordat. Having said this, however, it is equally important to point out that they are far more than essays produced by privately constituted groups of like-minded people. Rather, they carry with them a degree of authority, varying perhaps in each case, but deriving from the standing and character of the groups or commissions which produced them.

Thus, the World Council of Churches' document, *The Ordained Ministry in Ecumenical Perspective*,[1] revised and approved at Accra in 1974, although it is but a document seeking an ecumenical consensus, carries with it not only the weight of the WCC secretariat on Faith and Order, but also the authority of agreements reached already by Faith and Order Conferences of the World Council of Churches, the findings of which are incorporated in it.

Possibly a claim to the highest place on the list in this respect could be entered on behalf of the Canterbury Statement of the Anglican–Roman Catholic International Commission.[2] The reasons for advancing such a claim would derive from the fact that ARCIC is appointed by the highest authorities in both communions and deliberately constituted on a world-wide basis as to its membership. Furthermore, it is a direct result of an official meeting between church leaders who announced in a common Declaration their intention of taking such a specific step with a view to the ultimate reconciliation of the two communions.

The fact is of course, that in examining this matter of documentary status we are not awarding places or positions, but reminding ourselves that there are gradations here which could conceivably have bearing on a particular document's range or impact.

The Lutheran–Roman Catholic document[3] comes from a nationally-constituted group in the United States, but one notes that it is published under the joint aegis of the Representatives of the USA National Committee of the Lutheran World Federation and the Bishops' Committee for Ecumenical and Interreligious Affairs.[4]

Nevertheless, this document has wider than national implications in that its submissions (35, 54) recommend mutual recognition of ministry and eucharist, and lest we should think that this is just a New World Symphony, unsuitable for European ears, grown insensitive through the habituations of history, we might recall that at the end of 1973 limited eucharistic sharing was officially permitted for Roman Catholics and Lutherans in Alsace and Lorraine by the Bishop of Strasbourg and by the Consistory of the Lutheran Church in that area.[5]

The work of the Group of Les Dombes results from the deliberations of a gathering of Roman Catholic and Protestant theologians in France, unofficial no doubt, but carrying with it since 1937 the authority of its great founder, the Abbé Paul Couturier, who guided the group with his intuition of the complementarity[6] of elements of Catholic and Reformed doctrine and his glimpse of the level at which a higher synthesis could emerge. The work of this Group too has a wider context through the contacts of some of its members who belong to the WCC Faith and Order Commission and to the Vatican Secretariat for Unity[7] and, in the case of the agreement on eucharistic doctrine, by reason of the amount of material common to the agreements of the WCC and the Group of Les Dombes.

We have therefore before us a selection of documents, differing as to the degree of their official *imprimatur*, and which indicates a broad consensus in certain areas; this in turn varies in degree and content. By comparing their structure and material a second clarification of their nature and value can be made, since in this way their common ground and their dissimilarities, their convergences and divergences, can be assessed. Such an examination should enable us not only to evaluate the documents in themselves and in their relation to one another but, more important, it should furnish us with the basis for a judgement as to whether all or any of these statements constitute the beginning of reconciliation in this area which for so long has sharply divided the churches.[8]

For convenience, the documents are referred to by the following initials: WCC, LC, ARCIC, and D. Numbers in parentheses ( ) refer to the numbered paragraphs in the documents.

A STRUCTURAL COMPARISON

The following comparison is strictly one of structure and it does not cover all the aspects peculiar to each document such as, for example, the fact that WCC looks at the ordination of women and at clerical celibacy. It simply endeavours to discover, from an examination of structures, whether and how far the theological principles governing the four documents are shared principles. The comparison will, however, draw attention separately to specific practical recommendations in and deductions from the individual statements.

Structure here means far more than a lifeless framework, since it is a structure of theological principles which we are analysing, and these are life-creating, having themselves been evolved from the thinking of the living Church, from its ongoing experience of and expression of the faith once for all delivered. The faith does not develop, but we develop into it and constantly understand it afresh or receive new insights into some aspect of it. Thus one generation is led to a truth hitherto forgotten; another generation is guided to cast in a fresh mould what a previous age had formulated. Within this process, by which the Church unceasingly assimilates the apostolic faith which she proclaims in her teaching, life, and mission, there is a frequent redistribution of emphases created by the Spirit who guides into all the truth and by the needs of the Church itself, as succeeding generations of the people of God strive to live and express that faith in the idiom and circumstances of their own time and place. Though we are part of this process, yet we can discern something of it at work in various truths or principles which this Spirit-guided process has uncovered or rediscovered and reshaped in our times.

We can see quite clearly certain of these creative discoveries, or rediscoveries or re-emphases, which are common to these documents.

1

First among these emphases is that which insists that the starting-point is the Church,[9] for the whole priestly people of God has a ministry and this is the living context of the ministry of the ordained priesthood.[10]

Inseparably involved with and essential to this is the conviction that the ministry of the Church continues the ministry of Jesus Christ by proclamation, faith, and life. From his ministry all ministry derives and on it all ministry is patterned, and through the Spirit is effective in the service of God and man.[11]

These documents are concurring that the primary aspect of the reality of ministry is that the whole Church has a ministry expressed through 'a diversity of forms of ministerial service';[12] that all ministry is from Christ to the world through the Spirit, and that ordained ministry can only be clearly discerned in this perspective which is both vertical and horizontal in its spread. It is a specific charism operating within a whole range of charismata in the service of reconciliation. Ministry is neither a caste nor an autocracy and can only be truly understood in relation to Christ and to the priestly people, for ministry is service. In other words, to use a convenient type of theological shorthand, the essential and explicative context of ministry is at once Christological, pneumatological, and ecclesial.

This set of interlocking ideas, which may be regarded as virtually one concept, represents the first of these theological principles which were suggested earlier as constituting a structure for these documents, though there are definite variations in detail and in deductions as between the individual statements. The point is that this is one of the changed and change-creating presuppositions in the debate on ministry and, with others, its effects could be productive of altered attitudes and of action.[13]

2

Closely allied to this first element is the way in which the documents as a whole handle apostolicity and apostolic succession, for here too the starting-point is the Church and not ministerial pedigrees. The bite of this rediscovery is felt wherever there is a tendency towards an exclusivist concentration on a genealogical concept of episcopal consecration in apostolic succession as being solely or chiefly normative for ecclesial apostolicity. The various documents are far from discounting such a succession, especially in respect of continuity and unity, but see it as part of the whole, and an important part, for succession in office and in proclamation have been intimately linked from earliest times. What is perhaps deserving of comment is the emergence of what looks like a type of *plene esse* view of such a succession. It is not surprising to find WCC claiming that more and more churches 'are expressing willingness to see episcopacy as a *pre-eminent sign* of the apostolic succession of the whole Church in faith, life, and doctrine, and as such, something that ought to be striven for if absent'.[14] It is more striking to find D describing it as '*the fulness of the sign* of apostolic succession',[15] and LC using the expression '*a valuable sign* and aspect of apostolicity',[16] in view of the fact that Roman Catholics were participants in both sets of conversations. The Canterbury Statement's exposition of apostolic succession sees the bishops as 'representative of their Churches in fidelity to the teaching and mission of the apostles and (because they) are members of the episcopal college, their participation also ensures the historical continuity of this church with the apostolic Church and of its bishops with the original apostolic ministry'.[17] This apostolic succession of the local church derives its importance—and this is a vital factor in authentic ecclesiality (What is a true Church?)—from the apostolicity of the whole Church. This is defined in terms of faith, life, and commission: 'The Church is apostolic not only because its faith and life must reflect the witness to Jesus Christ given in the early Church by the apostles, but also because it is charged to continue in the apostles' commission to communicate to the world what it has received'.[18]

It is here in the underlining of a rediscovered reality, namely that 'the primary manifestation of apostolic succession is to be found in the life of the Church as a whole',[19] that the possibility begins to emerge of a lever which may yet help to free the log-jam.

How do the documents treat this ecclesial apostolicity and how do they relate to it an apostolic ministry and apostolic succession? Due to variations in the method of handling the whole theme of ministry, the weight of emphasis alters somewhat from document to document, but none would dispute what seem to be the key-sentences of WCC:

> The fullness of the apostolic succession of the whole Church involves continuity in the permanent characteristics of the Church of the apostles: witness to the apostolic faith, proclamation and fresh interpretation of the apostolic gospel, transmission of ministerial responsibility, sacramental life, community in love, service for the needy, unity among local churches, and sharing the gifts which the Lord has given to each.
>
> The ordained ministry is related in various degrees to all of these characteristics. It serves as an authorized and responsible instrument for their preservation and actualization. The orderly transmission of the ministry is, therefore, both a visible sign of this succession of the whole Church and of the effective participation of the ministry in it and contribution to it. Where this orderly transmission is lacking, a community must ask itself whether its apostolicity can be maintained in its fullness. Or, where this ministry does not adequately subserve the Church's apostolicity, a Church must ask itself whether or not its ministerial structures should continue with no alteration.[20]

The following section inserts into this context the episcopal succession which it variously describes as 'the predominant form of ministry (among others) in which the apostolicity of the Church was expressed'; 'an effective sign, not a guarantee, of the continuity of the Church in apostolic faith and mission', and as 'a pre-eminent sign of the apostolic succession of the whole

Church in faith, life and doctrine'. The section discusses the impossibility of showing that such a church order existed everywhere from the beginning, the difficulty created by identifying totally the episcopal succession and the apostolicity of the whole Church, and the effect of a growing agreement among scholars critical of some positions held hitherto.[21]

D describes the Church as 'apostolic in its very essence' and further notes that there is 'an apostolic succession of the whole Church' within which there is 'an apostolic succession in the ministry instituted by our Lord'.[22]

The statement then makes use of the expression 'the fulness of the apostolic succession' which it applies to the ecclesial and ministerial successions, defining its meaning in respect of each.[23] The difficulty which remains is that of the interpretation of the historic shapes assumed by the apostolic succession in the ministry of the different churches.[24] Part Two advocates recognition by both churches of 'the substantial reality' or 'the reality' of their respective ministries,[25] and proposes an act of reconciliation, submitting the suggestion to the authorities of the two churches. It is of interest that the Protestant submission states that 'we are deprived, not of the apostolic succession, but of the fulness of the sign of this succession', and asserts the necessity to return to it. The Roman Catholic side recognizes the apostolic succession in faith of the Reformed Churches and the efficacy of their ministry. The proposal then is 'to complete this recognition' by joining it 'to the normal sign of the episcopal succession which is indispensable, in Catholic doctrine, to the fulness of the ministry perfectly signified'.[26]

The terminology used by both sides—'fulness of the sign', 'normal sign', 'fulness of the ministry perfectly signified', 'to complete this recognition'—is obviously significant in its implications, which appear to fall under a general *plene esse* heading. D might be described as taking from WCC the phrase 'the fulness of the apostolic succession' and making its own of it.

The thrust of LC is in some ways different but the content is not: the ministry is apostolic and it is so within the apostolicity of the Church, for apostolicity is of doctrine, practices and authority, of proclamation and life. Doctrinal succession, which is of the essence, was from early times ensured by a succession in apostolic office.[27]

The concluding paragraph of the Common Observations is particularly interesting not only in itself, but as an assessment of apostolicity and in its awareness of the pressures of the times 'urging both the renewal of what is basic in our apostolic heritage as well as open-ness to the variants that our Christian witness to the world requires'.

The paragraph leads in with an agreement that 'These ways in which the Ministry has been structured and implemented in our two traditions appear to us to be consonant with apostolic teaching and practice. We are agreed that the basic reality of the apostolic ministry can be preserved amid variations in structure and implementation, in rites of ordination and in theological explanation'.[28]

When one turns to the separate reflections of both sets of participants, one finds this recognition recommended by each group to the authorities which appointed them.[29] It is noteworthy that what is proposed is a flat recognition on the grounds of agreement in apostolic faith and in the general soundness of each other's doctrine, practice, and piety, particularly in the areas of church, ministry, and eucharist. No service of reconciliation appears to be envisaged, or at least it is not suggested.

It should be noted that each set of participants issues cautions (33) and (59) which insist, from both sides, that there are still obstacles to intercommunion and eucharistic sharing. They might fairly be described as proposing possibilities which they approve and advocate for further consideration by their authorities.

What of episcopacy in relation to apostolicity? Episcopacy presents no problems for the Lutherans, not only because some of their churches have episcopacy 'in historic succession' and others have it 'without this succession', but also because the Lutheran reformers had desired to retain it if possible. But for them the retention of the ordained Ministry is the important thing. It is a *bene esse* view, if these labels are to be used at all.

The reflections of the Roman Catholic participants are equally interesting, particularly in respect of apostolicity in this connection. They maintain that the view which regards Lutheran churches as defective in apostolicity is only true 'if apostolicity is defined so as necessarily to include apostolic succession through episcopal consecration. However, it is dubious that apostolicity should be so defined'.[30]

The thrust of LC, both in the common and separate reflections, is towards gospel, creed, and sacrament preserving a form of apostolicity and towards the interplay here of doctrinal integrity and succession. Thus the Roman Catholic members insist that 'apostolic succession through episcopal consecration is a valuable sign and aspect of apostolicity'.[31] They 'are not in any way challenging' the insistence on episcopal ordination or suggesting that it be changed and they 'affirm explicitly that the apostolic Ministry is retained in a pre-eminent way in the episcopate, the presbyterate, and the diaconate. We would rejoice if episcopacy in apostolic succession, functioning as the effective sign of church unity, were acceptable to all, but we have envisaged a practical and immediate solution in a *de facto* situation where episcopacy is not yet seen in that light'.[32]

Probably its proponents would qualify with some legitimate refinements the comment that that recommendation implies a *plene esse* view, although its effects are the same and it resembles in its implications that view which regards episcopacy in succession as belonging to the perfection of a Church. In effect, it would seem to imply, and should be seen in conjunction with, *an ecclesiology of the unprecedented situation*.[33] Concepts, such as *ecclesia supplet* and the Orthodox idea of economy might also be felt to hover in the background.

Something has already been said about ARCIC's view of apostolicity and apostolic succession, and only it and LC draw attention to the different concepts of 'apostle' in the New Testament and to the implications of this.[34] Something further needs to be said about the Canterbury Statement, so at this stage we simply note ARCIC's phrase which draws together the various strands in apostolicity.[35] It spells out what apostolic succession means for the two communions, not saying too much or too little, and making no explicit reference to non-episcopal churches, for as a bilateral conversation this was not its business. It does assert the continuity of the local church with the apostolic Church and of its bishops with the original apostolic ministry, without claiming that that ministry was identical in *structure* with that of the second century. In this, it is in keeping with Vatican II and Bishop William Stubbs, one of the drafters of the Encyclical Letter of the Lambeth Conference 1888.[34]

We may note briefly some further principles which help to constitute a common structure for these modern documents on ministry.

3

Closely linked with 1 and 2 is the recognition of a plurality of ministerial forms in the New Testament and of the historical character of these patterns. Although they very quickly emerged as the threefold ministry, the difficulty of grounding in the New Testament any exclusive conception of Church order is recognized or implied in the documents.[37] At the same time there is in several of the documents the implication that to ignore the early emergence of monepiscopacy is, in a sense, to ignore the existence of the living Church, and there is the further explicit assertion of such a polity as 'agreeable to the Word of God' and an instrument of apostolicity.

4

A fourth principle common to these ecumenical documents on ministry is the acceptance that there is a sacramental reality involved in ordination.[38]

5

A fifth agreement is concerning the functions of the ministers as ministers of the word and sacraments. 'Since the ordained ministers are ministers of the gospel, every facet of their oversight is linked with the word of God', says the Canterbury Statement, and it adds 'The part of the ministers in the celebration of the sacraments is one with their responsibility for ministry of the word. In both word and sacrament Christians meet the living word of God' (10, 11). The ordained ministers build up and gather the community, leading and co-ordinating, promoting the Church's mission. They proclaim and show forth the news of reconciliation and preside over baptism and the eucharist, serving the priesthood of all the faithful. They serve and signify the unity of the local churches through time and in space.[39]

Within this framework of agreement, two points require notice: (*a*) the relation of the ordained ministry to the priesthood of all the baptized; (*b*) the priestly quality of the ordained ministry.

(*a*) As to the first; bearing in mind that most New Testament terms for ministerial leadership are functional,[40] and recalling that the emergence of terms such as status, order, estates, clergy, and laity, has been affected by cultural and sociological influences which have tended to conceal the theological concept that ministry is something shared by all Christians, what light do these documents throw?

It seems clear that, with a varying degree of emphasis, they concur that the ordained share in the ministry of the people of God but that 'their ministry is not an extension of the common priesthood but belongs to another realm of gifts of the Spirit'.[41] 'Ordination, the sign of a difference of charisms between the pastoral ministry and the priesthood of the baptized, far from separating ministers from God's people and making them a clerical caste, identifies them more fully with the life of the Church'.[42] It is 'a special order of Ministry' in the Church and 'has a special role within the ministry of the people of God', something distinct from the general ministry.[43]

The very term 'relationships' used by some of the documents implies this distinction within the whole community, a distinction which, however, is seen not in terms of grading but in terms of the calling, commissioning, and commitment in and through the Spirit for a particular range of service to the priestly people.[44]

(*b*) The second point which calls for comment is the question of the priesthood of the pastoral ministry.

LC recognizes that 'the whole Church has a priesthood in Christ' and that those who are united with him by baptism and faith are also 'united with, and share, his priesthood'.[45] While it does not discuss the concept of the priesthood of the ordained ministry specifically, the fact is there throughout the discussion of the nature of this ministry. WCC, like ARCIC, commenting on the absence of *hiereus* in the New Testament as a description of the ordained minister, notes that 'tradition has not been afraid of this usage'. The document stresses the need to discuss the term in the context of the search for reconciliation of ministries. It refers back the priestly function to the unique priesthood of Christ and to the common priesthood of the baptized, and it is interesting that it uses the term 'based upon' (cf. LC (10)), much as ARCIC uses the term 'reflects'. In other words, WCC does not use a term which suggests the complete identification of the priestly ministry of the ordained with Christ's priesthood or with the royal priesthood.

The document builds the priestly ministry of the ordained on the two concepts of sacrifice and intercession, linking them with the sacrifice and intercession of Christ and with the Christian's sacrifice and intercession.

As does Fr Jean Tillard, WCC insists that 'the ordained ministry is then of a completely new and different nature in relation to the sacrificial priesthood of the Old Testament'. It notes that 'the Minister, who participates, as every Christian, in the priesthood of Christ, and of all the people of God, fulfils his particular priestly service in strengthening, building up and expressing the royal and prophetic priesthood of the faithful through the service of the Gospel, the leading of the liturgical and sacramental life of the eucharistic community, and intercession'.

More specifically, D justifies the conviction that the pastoral ministry has a sacerdotal quality:

> Within the priesthood of the baptized, Christ gives his Church its structure, thanks to the pastoral ministry through which he leads his disciples to spiritual sacrifice, witness and service along many roads which, as it were, meet and cross in the Eucharist. It is in this sense that the ministry is said to be sacerdotal.[46]

Similar thinking to what lies behind these extracts is spelt out in the Canterbury Statement,[47] though with a somewhat different balance of emphases, and the reasons for this fuller treatment are historical as well as theological. Historically, one of the questions which has vexed Anglican/Roman Catholic relations is the complex of 'What is priesthood?' 'Who has it?' and 'How did he get it?' It had not always been so as may be seen, for example, from the correspondence of Archbishop Wake of Canterbury at the beginning of the eighteenth century with the French theologians, Girardin and Le Courayer. They accepted the validity of Anglican orders and Le Courayer's *Dissertation sur la Validité des Ordinations des Anglais et la Succession des Évêques de l'Église Anglicane* (1723) was a well-known book.[48] But with the publication of *Apostolicae Curae* in 1896 and the *Reply of the English Archbishops* in the following year, relations plummeted to their nadir.

The question then hinges on the nature of priesthood and the Statement agreed by ARCIC offers an answer sited within the context of the New Testament's teaching on ministry and having relevance to the problem as it faces the two churches, both of which are committed to the ministry of bishops, priests, and deacons.

ARCIC claims unequivocally that 'the development of the thinking in our two Communions regarding the nature of the Church and of the Ordained Ministry, as represented in our Statement, has, we consider, put these issues in a new context. Agreement on the nature of Ministry is prior to the consideration of the mutual recognition of ministries'.[49]

In effect, the old disagreement is largely bypassed, since in the light of a doctrine of ministry, shared to a noteworthy extent by the other documents under review, and which takes account of the evidence of the New Testament and of the early Church, much of it now appears irrelevant and misleading. The fact is that a very different picture of priesthood has now emerged and there is a converging trend here in both churches.

In this connection, the phrase 'as represented in our Statement' is important, since this trend towards a similar thinking on priesthood can be observed in such documents as the Report of the 1968 Lambeth Conference, the relevant paragraphs of *The Ministerial Priesthood* (1971) from the Synod of Bishops, and the Six Propositions with which the report of the *International Theological Commission* (1970) ended. In particular, the *Decree on the*

Ministry and Life of Priests of Vatican II demonstrates in many passages this new thinking (or is it the old thinking come back?) which, in Bishop Guilford C. Young's frank phrases corrects an off-balance view of priesthood and no longer focuses on the priest as the 'cult man'.[50] All this gives substance too to the conviction expressed in the preface to ARCIC 'that in what we have said here both Anglican and Roman Catholic will recognize their own faith'.

Compressed into ARCIC (13) are certain theological elements which create the picture of the priestly quality of ministry and which dictate its form and content.

1 The High Priesthood of Christ Jesus is unique. It continues on our behalf but in itself it is an intransmissible priesthood (*aparabatos*, Heb. 7. 24). No claim is made by ARCIC that the priestly role of the minister shares in Christ's High Priesthood, for this is incommunicable. It is noticeable too that, in connection with the priesthood of all Christians, neither does ARCIC use an unqualified phrase such as 'All Christians share in the priesthood of their Lord' (Lambeth 1968) or 'All the faithful in the Church are called to share in it' (Six Propositions, no. 2).[51] Rather does it imply that the 'royal priesthood' (1 Pet. 2. 9, 10) can offer the spiritual sacrifice of Christian living because of, and as a result of, the one perfect sacrifice of the unique High Priest. It might be better to say, with R. P. C. Hanson, that the priesthood of Christ is expressed by and reflected in the Church as a priestly body.[52]

2 Closely linked with the first element is the priestly vocation of the whole Church, that of 'self-offering to God as a living sacrifice (Rom. 12. 1)'. The continuing mission of the Church is 'to proclaim reconciliation in Christ and to manifest his reconciling love' (ARCIC 12). The eucharist is the 'memorial of the totality of God's reconciling action in Christ' (13, and cf. 12.) The Church is 'this reconciling community' (5) and the ordained minister is 'an authoritative representative of Christ and proclaims his message of reconciliation' (8). Gospel, Church and Ministry are inseparably linked by the concept of reconciliation:

From first to last this has been the work of God. He has reconciled us men to himself through Christ, and he has enlisted us in this service of reconciliation. What I mean is, that God was in Christ reconciling the world to himself, no longer holding men's misdeeds against them, and that he has entrusted us with the message of reconciliation. We come therefore as Christ's ambassadors. It is as if God were appealing to you through us: in Christ's name, we implore you, be reconciled to God (2 Cor. 5. 18–20).

3 If it is not derived from Christ's incommunicable High Priesthood, and if it 'is not an extension of the common Christian Priesthood' (13), how is this service of reconciliation a priestly ministry? If its goal is 'to serve this priesthood of all the faithful' and 'to help the Church to be a royal priesthood' (7, 13), what do Anglicans and Roman Catholics see as the justification for their use of 'priestly terms in speaking about the ordained ministry'? (13). The Canterbury Statement uses the word 'reflects'; 'Christians came to see the priestly rôle of Christ reflected in these ministers' (13). As the eucharist bears a sacramental relation to the sacrifice of the one High Priest, so priestly terms came to be used of the minister presiding at the *memorial* of that one sacrifice, since his action 'is seen to stand in a sacramental relation to what Christ himself did in offering his own sacrifice' (13). In the words of Jean Tillard, it is 'a priesthood *sui generis*, wholly relative to the unique priestly act of Jesus'.[53]

The Statement also uses the word 'representative' (8, 13), a term which is widely used in other documents in this connection.[54] Emphasizing that the ministers represent Christ to the world and, in the offering of worship, the Church before God, Hanson writes:

It is a priesthood central to, and representative of, the Church, not external to it, a priesthood which concentrates and expresses within the Church the priestly function which the whole Church corporately possesses because it is united with Christ, the High Priest *par excellence*. In whatever sense the eucharist may be said to be a sacrifice this priesthood offers this sacrifice along with and in the midst of and representatively for the whole Church. This concept of priesthood might be said indeed to be agreeable to Scripture.[55]

Not only in these respects is there a priestly service but also in 'effectively proclaiming the gospel'[56] and thus helping 'the Church to be a royal priesthood' through fulfilling its vocation 'of self-offering . . . as a living sacrifice' (13). One may compare D (31) and WCC (21-2) and trace the origins of this thinking to Rom. 15. 16:

His grace has made me a minister (*leitourgon*) of Christ Jesus to the Gentiles; my priestly service (*hierourgounta*) is the preaching of the Gospel of God, and it falls to me to offer the Gentiles to him as an acceptable sacrifice (*prosphora*), consecrated by the Holy Spirit.

The comment of St John Chrysostom on the passage is apposite:

My priesthood is to preach and announce the Gospel, this is the sacrifice which I offer.

POSTSCRIPT

It is no part of a documentary analysis such as this to broach the wider question of where the movement for Christian unity is going and how it is trying to reach its objective. All it should do by way of conclusion is to indicate that these four documents relate directly to the basic fact of separation, namely, that not all Christians feel able, for a variety of reasons, to break the eucharistic bread together. In this situation there enter not only the question of the conditions necessary for intercommunion, but the role, function, and authority of the minister of the eucharist, and ultimately the nature of the Church itself.

Ecumenism and union plans are not at the moment having a particularly good press. Many people are impatient for visible results and *de facto* intercommunion could become an increasingly common feature. Others have tended to lose heart and interest.

A radical solution would be to authorize general intercommunion without tarrying for any. A possible strength of such a view might be the claim that *total* agreement on eucharistic doctrine is very unlikely and that disagreements even at a deep level should be tolerated. A weakness could be that this approach, though by no means intending to do so, could, as far as results go, have the *effect* of a soft option. People could treat such intercommunion as an end in itself and the goal could turn out to be nothing more than an extended version of the *status quo* of separation. For some, this would be enough and they would describe the result in more positive terms.

This type of answer does not lie behind the four documents yet it has been obvious that some of them favour occasional intercommunion in specific circumstances while others look towards more general intercommunion when certain problems are cleared up. ARCIC takes the line that a *substantial* agreement on the eucharist and agreement on the essentials of ministry are prior to reconciliation of ministries and that a consensus should be first sought. In other words, it looks towards full communion. Yet the pressures of separation are being felt more and more. Bishop Alan C. Clark's comment refers to 'the scarcely veiled pressure for some solution to the vexed question of intercommunion. Whereas theological precision would argue against it, the concrete situation, some feel, would argue for a modicum of exceptional practice. At the same time no suggestion is made for any unilateral initiative without the consent of church authority'.[57] The 1973 Report of the Anglican Consultative Council contains a sentence of similar meaning: 'The co-operation of Christians is now in a phase which cries out for intercommunion'. In a sympathetic review of the situation the Report continues. 'But local intercommunion may lead to confusion and even sectarianism unless there are more than local approaches to the unifying of ministries and churches'. It concludes: 'We reaffirm the conviction that organic union in the sense of united Churches is a goal for which intercommunion alone or federation is no substitute'.[58] In this it reflects Resolution 47 of the Lambeth Conference of 1968 and its section report. Reciprocal acts of intercommunion should be between churches seeking 'unity in a way which includes agreement on apostolic faith and order, and where that agreement . . . has found expression, whether in a covenant to unite or in some other appropriate form. . .'. Such intercommunion 'should be regarded as only a temporary relationship on the way to organic union'. The same section report adds, 'Whenever intercommunion is proposed between Churches we believe that there should first be found a basic agreement on the meaning of the eucharist'.[59] It should however be noted that Lambeth 1968 also passed a resolution (no. 45) permitting other Christians to communicate in Anglican churches and the section report (no. III) spelt out the details. It did so, 'keeping the goal of full communion in view' and 'in order to meet special pastoral needs of God's people, under the direction of the bishop'.

The quest for consensus is a rigorous and demanding exercise and it is broadly speaking the line followed by ARCIC and by many reunion schemes. Its proponents regard it as basically more realistic than the approach represented by those who favour open or free communion and couple with it some form of the concept of intercommunion as a goal in itself. (See paras. 160 and 161 in the report *Intercommunion Today*.)[60]

There is wisdom in the section of WCC (90-1) dealing with the unity of the Church and the recognition of ministries:

> The sign of the apostolic succession has become a major factor of disunity in the latter cases. It follows that mutual recognition cannot be achieved in the same way between all churches. While in some conversations the emphasis must be laid on matters of faith which divide, in others attention must centre on the understanding of the ministry itself.
>
> A common understanding of the ministry will thus not have the same effect on all relations between the divided churches. This question is certainly of vital importance for all churches, and it is clear that without a common understanding no decisive progress can be made on the road towards unity. But while for some churches a common view and practice of the ministry will not immediately change the situation, for others they would represent the breakthrough which is required.

It may well be that all concerned should look more closely at the real possibility of an interim stage, that of partial communion between churches which have formally agreed on apostolic faith and order and which have set a course together for unity. This would take into account the overall relationship between the churches concerned and the need for experiencing at all levels the process of growing together.

Should there not also be called into play here two other concepts, that of unity by stages and that of a sound pluralism? On the first of these the preparatory statement on the ministry document by the co-chairmen of ARCIC says:

> It is relevant to recall that the Malta Report of the Anglican–Roman Catholic Joint Preparatory Commission saw this process of inter-Church reconciliation in terms of stages. It is a step-by-step process in which the achievement of this kind of consensus is an essential element.
>
> As the commission produces its agreed statements on eucharist and on ministry it is then for both communions to decide if a situation is being created which fosters and promotes the reconciliation of our Churches and demands from them appropriate action.[61]

On the second point, that of 'welcoming a sound pluralism in our exposition of Catholic faith' (the phrase is Fr Jean Tillard's) we have to take account, as he says, of the fact that 'this pluralism already exists, even on points of considerable importance'. He remarks that certain 'lines of cleavage are in fact frequently found *within* each Church',[62] a point not neglected in both the ARCIC Statements.[63] This aspect of the total situation is examined in two important papers, the first by Cardinal J. C. M. Willebrands and the second by Bishop J. R. H. Moorman and Professor Howard E. Root, in the published account of the Preparatory Commission's work.[64] In these papers the questions of unity and comprehensiveness and of the legitimate limits of diversity in a united church were discussed.

There unfolds before separated Christians a pattern of alternatives from which sooner rather than later choices will have to be made. Generally speaking, these four documents have a common method and objective, although significant variations have been noted as between some of them. Behind them all lie inter-Church co-operation and contacts, joint research and shared experience, which apart from the documents themselves are a measure of progress to be reckoned against the inevitable setbacks. They are interim documents, parts of a process to which they are contributions; and whatever the stages on the way and the methods favoured, they are directed towards the organic reality of 'one bread, one body'.

NOTES

References to pages in this book are in brackets, thus [ ].

1. [pp. 111–41]
2. [pp. 29–49]
3. [pp. 53–86]
4. The disclaimer in their Foreword [pp. 53–4] that 'It must again be emphasized that the studies and position papers contained herein represent the views of the authors and of the dialogue groups, and do not constitute official statements by any of the Churches of which they are members' has to be taken in conjunction with the assertion, 'the common statement of the group, adopted unanimously, together with the separate statements of the representatives of the two traditions represent a forward step of immense significance'. (Ibid.)
5. See report in *Church Times*, 18 January 1974.
6. Cf. D (39) [p. 102]
7. See the introduction to the Group's *Towards a Common Eucharistic Faith?* in *Modern Eucharistic Agreement* (SPCK), pp. 54–5.
8. Cf. WCC (93)–(106), [pp. 137–41]
9. Cf. *Anglican-Roman Catholic Dialogue: The Work of the Preparatory Commission* (Oxford 1974), p. 50 (E. R. Fairweather); p. 98 (H. R. McAdoo).
10. Cf. WCC (2) [p. 111]; LC (9)–(11) [pp. 57–8]; ARCIC (2), (7) [p. 30, 32]; D (5) (9), (14)–(19) [pp. 95–7]
11. WCC (3–12) [pp. 111–14], and cf. D (5)–(7) [p. 94]; LC (6)–(10) [pp. 56–7]; ARCIC (3), (10) [pp. 30, 33]
12. ARCIC (2) [p. 30]
13. Note LC Foreword 'The common statement of the group, adopted unanimously, together with the separate statements of the representatives of the two traditions *represent a forward step of immense significance*' [p. 54]

14. WCC (37) [pp. 121]
15. D (13), (40), (43) [pp. 96, 103, 104]
16. LC (44) [p. 70]
17. ARCIC (16) [p. 36]
18. ARCIC (4) [p. 31]
19. WCC (27) [p. 118]
20. WCC (28)–(29) [p. 119]
21. WCC (30)–(37) [pp. 119–21]
22. D (8)–(11) [p. 95]
23. D (12), (13) [pp. 95–6]
24. D (37) [pp. 100–01]
25. D (40), (43) [pp. 103, 104]
26. D (40)–(47) [pp. 103–5]
27. LC (12)–(18) [pp. 58–60]
28. LC (22) [p. 61]
29. LC (35), (54) [pp. 66, 74]
30. LC (44) [p. 70]
31. Ibid.
32. LC (57) [p. 75]
33. See, for example, D. J. O'Hanlon 'A New Approach to the Validity of Church Orders', in *Worship* (vol. 42, no. 7).
34. ARCIC 4 [p. 31] and LC (Roman Catholic Observations), (38) [p. 68]
35. Ibid. (16): 'Moreover, because they are representative of their churches in fidelity to the teaching and mission of the apostles and are members of the episcopal college, their participation also ensures the historical continuity of this church with the apostolic church and of its bishops with the original apostolic ministry.'
36. Vatican II contents itself with saying that the ecclesiastical ministry is exercised on different levels by those who *from antiquity* have been called bishops, priests, and deacons. (For discussion, see Hans Küng, *The Church*, pp. 417–18). Stubbs speaks of the 'historic episcopate' as 'a distinct, substantive, and historic transmission of the commission of the apostles in and by which our Lord formed his disciples into a distinctly organized body or Church' (*Christian Unity: The Anglican Position* (1948); ed. G. K. A. Bell, p. 180.)
37. WCC (31) [pp. 119–20]; LC (11), (14), (20), (38), (40) [pp. 57, 58, 60, 68, 69]; ARCIC (5), (6) [pp. 31–2] and D by implication
38. WCC (44)–(46) [pp. 123–4], LC (16) (50) [pp. 61, 76]; ARCIC (14), (15) and n. 4 [p. 37]; D (35) [p. 100]

39. WCC (14), (15), (45) [pp. 114–15, 124]; LC (12), (13) [p. 58]; ARCIC (7)–(9) [p. 32–3]; D (25)–(31) [pp. 98–9]

40. WCC (39)–(42) [p. 122–3]

41. ARCIC (13) and cf. (14) [p. 35]

42. D (36) [p. 100] and cf. (11), (21), (24, 30)

43. LC (13), (19), (49) [pp. 58, 60, 71–2]

44. Cf. WCC (7), (9), (15) [pp. 112, 113, 115]; D (30) [p. 99]

45. LC (10) [p. 57]

46. WCC (21)–(22) [pp. 116–17]; D (31) [p. 99] and cf. the Preamble [p. 90]

47. ARCIC (13) [pp. 34–5]

48. See *William Wake, Archbishop of Canterbury (1657–1737)*, by Norman Sykes (Cambridge 1957), vol. I, pp. 315–66.

49. ARCIC (17) [p. 36]

50. *The Lambeth Conference 1968*, Resolution 31 and Report of Section II, particularly *Priesthood*, pp. 100–02; *The Ministerial Priesthood* (Vatican 1971); Part I (4); Report of the International Theological Commission, 10 October 1970, on 'The Priestly Ministry' (Paris 1971); *The Documents of Vatican II;* ed. W. M. Abbott, pp. 526–76

51. Cf. *A Plan of Union* (First Draft), 1972, pp. 24–5 (Church Unity Commission, Braamfontein, Transvaal, South Africa). Stating that 'Christ alone is the true priest' and that 'all Christians share in the priesthood of Christ as members of his Body', it also notes 'The Church is that part of mankind which has responded to the call of God and has been strengthened and cleansed by his grace to work for the salvation of the whole world. *To this extent the Church shares the priestly ministry of Christ'*.

52. R. P. C. Hanson, *Groundwork for Unity* (1971), p. 47, and cf. Jean M. R. Tillard, *What Priesthood has the Ministry?* (Grove Booklet No. 13, 1973)

53. *What Priesthood has the Ministry?* p. 27: 'We have rather to do with a priesthood *sui generis*, wholly relative to the unique priestly act of Jesus, intended to assure the contact of the community with that act in the *hic et nunc*. This priesthood only yields up its meaning when read in the light of the *Memorial* (in the technical sense of the term) which is the sacramental mirror reflecting *hic et nunc* to the Church the event of the Passover of Christ. Thanks to this priesthood the community can sit at the table where the sacrificial death of the unique priest is celebrated.'

54. See *Conversations between the Church of England and the Methodist Church*, p. 23; it 'acts representatively and in conjunction with the laity's exercise of its priesthood'; it 'represents Christ before the

community and at its head' (*Six Propositions*, no. 4); 'The relationship of the ministerial priesthood or ordained ministry to the general Priesthood may be expressed in terms of representation', and 'by virtue of his ordination he acts as the representative both of the general priesthood and of Christ' (South African *Plan of Union*, pp. 25–6), and cp. *Lambeth Report 1968*, pp. 100–01.

55. Op. cit., pp. 47–8
56. *The Ministerial Priesthood*, Part I, 4; and cf. *Six Propositions*, no. 3: 'The episcopal and presbyteral ministry is therefore sacerdotal in the sense that it makes present Christ's service in effective proclamation of the gospel message, in the gathering and direction of the Christian community, the remission of sins and the eucharistic celebration, where Christ's unique sacrifice is in a special way made effective in the present'; and *Documents of Vatican II, Decree on the Ministry and Life of Priests*, C. I, 4.
57. Foreword to *Modern Eucharistic Agreement* (1973)
58. *Partners in Mission*, Anglican Consultative Council, Second Meeting, Dublin, 1973, pp. 2–4
59. *Report of Lambeth Conference 1968*, pp. 42, 128
60. *Intercommunion Today* (1968), p. 94
61. Presentation of 'Ministry and Ordination: A Statement on the Doctrine of the Ministry' by the Co-Chairmen (released 13 December 1973) and cf. *Anglican/Roman Catholic Dialogue* (1974); ed. Alan C. Clark and Colin Davey, pp. 84–106
62. 'Roman Catholics and Anglicans: the Eucharist', in *One in Christ* 1973, vol. IX, no. 2, pp. 132–3
63. Windsor Statement (12) and Canterbury Statement (Preface)
64. *Anglican/Roman Catholic Dialogue* (1974), pp. 37–83. See also 'Doctrinal Agreement and Christian Unity', a statement by the Anglican-Roman Catholic Consultation in the United States (1972), published in *Theology* (April 1972), vol. LXXV, no. 622.

MINISTRY AND ORDINATION

A Statement on the Doctrine of the Ministry Agreed by the Anglican–Roman Catholic International Commission

CANTERBURY 1973

First published 1973
by SPCK

© H. R. McAdoo, Bishop of Ossory, Ferns, and Leighlin
Alan C. Clark, Auxiliary Bishop of Northampton, 1973

PREFACE

At Windsor, in 1971, the Anglican–Roman Catholic International Commission was able to achieve an Agreed Statement on Eucharistic Doctrine. In accordance with the programme adopted at Venice in 1970 we have now, at our meeting in Canterbury in 1973, turned our attention to the doctrine of Ministry, specifically to our understanding of the Ordained Ministry and its place in the life of the Church. The present document is the result of the work of this officially appointed Commission and is offered to our authorities for their consideration. At this stage it remains an agreed statement of the Commission and no more.

We acknowledge with gratitude our debt to the many studies and discussions which have treated the same material. While respecting the different forms that Ministry has taken in other traditions, we hope that the clarification of our understanding expressed in the statement will be of service to them also.

We have submitted the statement, therefore, to our authorities and, with their authorization, we publish it as a document of the Commission with a view to its discussion. Even though there may be differences of emphasis within our two traditions, yet we believe that in what we have said here both Anglican and Roman Catholic will recognize their own faith.

H. R. McADOO, *Bishop of Ossory*
ALAN C. CLARK, *Bishop of Elmham*
CO-CHAIRMEN

THE STATEMENT

INTRODUCTION

1. Our intention has been to seek a deeper understanding of Ministry which is consonant with biblical teaching and with the traditions of our common inheritance, and to express in this document the consensus we have reached.[1] This statement is not designed to be an exhaustive treatment of Ministry. It seeks to express our basic agreement in the doctrinal areas that have been the source of controversy between us, in the wider context of our common convictions about the ministry.

2. Within the Roman Catholic Church and the Anglican Communion there exists a diversity of forms of ministerial service. Of more specific ways of service, while some are undertaken without particular initiative from official authority, others may receive a mandate from ecclesiastical authorities. The ordained ministry can only be rightly understood within this broader context of various ministries, all of which are the work of one and the same Spirit.

MINISTRY IN THE LIFE OF THE CHURCH

3. The life and self-offering of Christ perfectly express what it is to serve God and man. All Christian ministry, whose purpose is always to build up the community (*koinonia*), flows and takes its shape from this source and model. The communion of men with God (and with each other) requires their reconciliation. This reconciliation, accomplished by the death and resurrection of Jesus Christ, is being realized in the life of the Church through the response of faith. While the Church is still in process of sanctification, its mission is nevertheless to be the instrument by which this reconciliation in Christ is proclaimed, his love manifested, and the means of salvation offered to men.

4. In the early Church the apostles exercised a ministry which remains of fundamental significance for the Church of all ages.

It is difficult to deduce, from the New Testament use of 'apostle' for the Twelve, Paul, and others, a precise portrait of an apostle, but two primary features of the original apostolate are clearly discernible: a special relationship with the historical Christ, and a commission from him to the Church and the world (Matt. 28. 19; Mark 3.14). All Christian apostolate originates in the sending of the Son by the Father. The Church is apostolic not only because its faith and life must reflect the witness to Jesus Christ given in the early Church by the apostles, but also because it is charged to continue in the apostles' commission to communicate to the world what it has received. Within the whole history of mankind the Church is to be the community of reconciliation.

5. All ministries are used by the Holy Spirit for the building up of the Church to be this reconciling community for the glory of God and the salvation of men (Eph. 4. 11–13). Within the New Testament ministerial actions are varied and functions not precisely defined. Explicit emphasis is given to the proclamation of the Word and the preservation of apostolic doctrine, the care of the flock, and the example of Christian living. At least by the time of the Pastoral Epistles and 1 Peter, some ministerial functions are discernible in a more exact form. The evidence suggests that with the growth of the Church the importance of certain functions led to their being located in specific officers of the community. Since the Church is built up by the Holy Spirit primarily but not exclusively through these ministerial functions, some form of recognition and authorization is already required in the New Testament period for those who exercise them in the name of Christ. Here we can see elements which will remain at the heart of what today we call ordination.

6. The New Testament shows that ministerial office played an essential part in the life of the Church in the first century, and we believe that the provision of a ministry of this kind is part of God's design for his people. Normative principles governing the purpose and function of the ministry are already present in the New Testament documents (e.g. Mark 10. 43–5; Acts 20. 28; 1 Tim. 4. 12–16; 1 Pet. 5. 1–4). The early churches may well

have had considerable diversity in the structure of pastoral ministry, though it is clear that some churches were headed by ministers who were called *episcopoi* and *presbyteroi*. While the first missionary churches were not a loose aggregation of autonomous communities, we have no evidence that bishops and 'presbyters' were appointed everywhere in the primitive period. The terms 'bishop' and 'presbyter' could be applied to the same man or to men with identical or very similar functions. Just as the formation of the canon of the New Testament was a process incomplete until the second half of the second century, so also the full emergence of the threefold ministry of bishop, presbyter, and deacon required a longer period than the apostolic age. Thereafter this three-fold structure became universal in the Church.

THE ORDAINED MINISTRY

7. The Christian community exists to give glory to God through the fulfilment of the Father's purpose. All Christians are called to serve this purpose by their life of prayer and surrender to divine grace, and by their careful attention to the needs of all human beings. They should witness to God's compassion for all mankind and his concern for justice in the affairs of men. They should offer themselves to God in praise and worship, and devote their energies to bringing men into the fellowship of Christ's people, and so under his rule of love. The goal of the ordained ministry is to serve this priesthood of all the faithful. Like any human community the Church requires a focus of leadership and unity, which the Holy Spirit provides in the ordained ministry. This ministry assumes various patterns to meet the varying needs of those whom the Church is seeking to serve, and it is the role of the minister to co-ordinate the activities of the Church's fellowship and to promote what is necessary and useful for the Church's life and mission. He is to discern what is of the Spirit in the diversity of the Church's life and promote its unity.

8. In the New Testament a variety of images is used to describe the functions of this minister. He is servant, both of Christ and of the Church. As herald and ambassador he is an authoritative

representative of Christ and proclaims his message of reconciliation. As teacher he explains and applies the word of God to the community. As shepherd he exercises pastoral care and guides the flock. He is a steward who may only provide for the household of God what belongs to Christ. He is to be an example both in holiness and in compassion.

9. An essential element in the ordained ministry is its responsibility for 'oversight' (*episcope*). This responsibility involves fidelity to the apostolic faith, its embodiment in the life of the Church today, and its transmission to the Church of tomorrow. Presbyters are joined with the bishop in his oversight of the church and in the ministry of the word and the sacraments; they are given authority to preside at the eucharist and to pronounce absolution. Deacons, although not so empowered, are associated with bishops and presbyters in the ministry of word and sacrament, and assist in oversight.

10. Since the ordained ministers are ministers of the gospel, every facet of their oversight is linked with the word of God. In the original mission and witness recorded in Holy Scripture lies the source and ground of their preaching and authority. By the preaching of the word they seek to bring those who are not Christians into the fellowship of Christ. The Christian message needs also to be unfolded to the faithful, in order to deepen their knowledge of God and their response of grateful faith. But a true faith calls for beliefs that are correct and lives that endorse the gospel. So the ministers have to guide the community and to advise individuals with regard to the implications of commitment to Christ. Because God's concern is not only for the welfare of the Church but also for the whole of creation, they must also lead their communities in the service of humanity. Church and people have continually to be brought under the guidance of the apostolic faith. In all these ways a ministerial vocation implies a responsibility for the word of God supported by constant prayer (cf. Acts 6. 4).

11. The part of the ministers in the celebration of the sacraments is one with their responsibility for ministry of the word. In both

word and sacrament Christians meet the living Word of God. The responsibility of the ministers in the Christian community involves them in being not only the persons who normally administer baptism, but also those who admit converts to the communion of the faithful and restore those who have fallen away. Authority to pronounce God's forgiveness of sin, given to bishops and presbyters at their ordination, is exercised by them to bring Christians to a closer communion with God and with their fellow men through Christ and to assure them of God's continuing love and mercy.

12. To proclaim reconciliation in Christ and to manifest his reconciling love belong to the continuing mission of the Church. The central act of worship, the eucharist, is the memorial of that reconciliation and nourishes the Church's life for the fulfilment of its mission. Hence it is right that he who has oversight in the church and is the focus of its unity should preside at the celebration of the eucharist. Evidence as early as Ignatius shows that at least in some churches, the man exercising this oversight presided at the eucharist and no other could do so without his consent (*Letter to the Smyrnaeans*, 8. 1).

13. The priestly sacrifice of Jesus was unique, as is also his continuing High Priesthood. Despite the fact that in the New Testament ministers are never called 'priests' (*hiereis*),[2] Christians came to see the priestly role of Christ reflected in these ministers and used priestly terms in describing them. Because the eucharist is the memorial of the sacrifice of Christ, the action of the presiding minister in reciting again the words of Christ at the Last Supper and distributing to the assembly the holy gifts is seen to stand in a sacramental relation to what Christ himself did in offering his own sacrifice. So our two traditions commonly use priestly terms in speaking about the ordained ministry. Such language does not imply any negation of the once-for-all sacrifice of Christ by any addition or repetition. There is in the eucharist a memorial (*anamnesis*)[3] of the totality of God's reconciling action in Christ, who through his minister presides at the Lord's supper and gives himself sacramentally. So it is because the eucharist is central in the Church's life that the essential nature of the Christian ministry,

however this may be expressed, is most clearly seen in its celebration; for, in the eucharist, thanksgiving is offered to God, the gospel of salvation is proclaimed in word and sacrament, and the community is knit together as one body in Christ. Christian ministers are members of this redeemed community. Not only do they share through baptism in the priesthood of the people of God, but they are—particularly in presiding at the eucharist—representative of the whole Church in the fulfilment of its priestly vocation of self-offering to God as a living sacrifice (Rom. 12. 1). Nevertheless their ministry is not an extension of the common Christian priesthood but belongs to another realm of the gifts of the Spirit. It exists to help the Church to be 'a royal priesthood, a holy nation, God's own people, to declare the wonderful deeds of him who called [them] out of darkness into his marvellous light' (1 Pet. 2. 9, RSV).

VOCATION AND ORDINATION

14. Ordination denotes entry into this apostolic and God-given ministry, which serves and signifies the unity of the local churches in themselves and with one another. Every individual act of ordination is therefore an expression of the continuing apostolicity and catholicity of the whole Church. Just as the original apostles did not choose themselves but were chosen and commissioned by Jesus, so those who are ordained are called by Christ in the Church and through the Church. Not only is their vocation from Christ but their qualification for exercising such a ministry is the gift of the Spirit: 'Our sufficiency is from God, who has qualified us to be ministers of a new covenant, not in a written code but in the Spirit' (2 Cor. 3. 5–6, RSV). This is expressed in ordination, when the bishop prays God to grant the gift of the Holy Spirit and lays hands on the candidate as the outward sign of the gifts bestowed. Because ministry is in and for the community and because ordination is an act in which the whole Church of God is involved, this prayer and laying on of hands takes place within the context of the eucharist.

15. In this sacramental act,[4] the gift of God is bestowed upon the ministers, with the promise of divine grace for their work and

for their sanctification; the ministry of Christ is presented to them as a model for their own; and the Spirit seals those whom he has chosen and consecrated. Just as Christ has united the Church inseparably with himself, and as God calls all the faithful to lifelong discipleship, so the gifts and calling of God to the ministers are irrevocable. For this reason, ordination is unrepeatable in both our churches.

16. Both presbyters and deacons are ordained by the bishop. In the ordination of a presbyter the presbyters present join the bishop in the laying on of hands, thus signifying the shared nature of the commission entrusted to them. In the ordination of a new bishop, other bishops lay hands on him, as they request the gift of the Spirit for his ministry and receive him into their ministerial fellowship. Because they are entrusted with the oversight of other churches, this participation in his ordination signifies that this new bishop and his church are within the communion of churches. Moreover, because they are representative of their churches in fidelity to the teaching and mission of the apostles and are members of the episcopal college, their participation also ensures the historical continuity of this church with the apostolic church and of its bishop with the original apostolic ministry. The communion of the churches in mission, faith, and holiness, through time and space, is thus symbolized and maintained in the bishop. Here are comprised the essential features of what is meant in our two traditions by ordination in the apostolic succession.

CONCLUSION

17. We are fully aware of the issues raised by the judgement of the Roman Catholic Church on Anglican Orders. The development of the thinking in our two Communions regarding the nature of the Church and of the Ordained Ministry, as represented in our Statement, has, we consider, put these issues in a new context. Agreement on the nature of Ministry is prior to the consideration of the mutual recognition of ministries. What we have to say represents the consensus of the Commission on essential matters where it considers that doctrine admits no divergence. It will be clear that we have not yet broached the

wide-ranging problems of authority which may arise in any discussion of Ministry, nor the question of primacy. We are aware that present understanding of such matters remains an obstacle to the reconciliation of our churches in the one Communion we desire, and the Commission is now turning to the examination of the issues involved. Nevertheless we consider that our consensus, on questions where agreement is indispensable for unity, offers a positive contribution to the reconciliation of our churches and of their ministries.

NOTES

1. Cf. *An Agreed Statement on Eucharistic Doctrine*, para. 1, which similarly speaks of a consensus reached with regard to the Eucharist.
2. In the English language the word 'priest' is used to translate two distinct Greek words, *hiereus* which belongs to the cultic order and *presbyteros* which designates an elder in the community.
3. Cf. *An Agreed Statement on Eucharistic Doctrine*, para. 5
4. Anglican use of the word 'sacrament' with reference to ordination is limited by the distinction drawn in the Thirty-nine Articles (Article 25) between the two 'sacraments of the Gospel' and the 'five commonly called sacraments'. Article 25 does not deny these latter the name 'sacrament', but differentiates between them and the 'two sacraments ordained by Christ' described in the Catechism as 'necessary to salvation' for all men.

APPENDIX
The Anglican–Roman Catholic International Commission's Discussion of the Doctrine of the Ministry
by Colin Davey

THIS APPENDIX WAS WRITTEN
AT THE REQUEST OF THE COMMISSION
BUT CARRIES ONLY THE AUTHORITY OF THE
CO-CHAIRMEN AND THE WRITER

In 1966 Pope Paul VI and the Archbishop of Canterbury announced their intention of inaugurating 'a serious dialogue founded on the Gospels and on the ancient common traditions' in the hope that this might 'lead to that unity in truth for which Christ prayed'.[1] The conversations between the Anglican and Roman Catholic theologians who have engaged in this dialogue have been in two stages. In 1967 and 1968 the Anglican–Roman Catholic Joint Preparatory Commission met 'to draw up a programme and establish priorities in the theological dialogue, as well as considering matters of practical ecclesiastical co-operation'.[2] From January 1970 onwards the Anglican–Roman Catholic International Commission has been meeting to discuss the subjects selected by the Preparatory Commission. At its first meeting the International Commission decided, on the basis of the recommendations made in the Preparatory Commission's 'Malta Report', that the three subjects on which its attention should first be concentrated were: *Eucharist, Ministry,* and *Authority*.

In discussing these the Commission's aim has been to see whether it is possible to 'find a way of advancing together beyond the doctrinal disagreements of the past' to a point where these doctrines 'will no longer constitute an obstacle to the unity we seek'.³ Its method has been to re-examine these questions in the light both of 'biblical teaching and the tradition of our common inheritance'⁴ and of 'the development of the thinking in our two Communions'⁵ about them. Within such a study, the members of the Commission have also asked themselves and each other, What is our faith on this point? What is our understanding of this doctrine? By asking and answering such questions it has proved possible for the Commission to discover 'a convergence of testimonies',⁶ and to express in its Agreed Statements a true consensus 'on essential matters where it considers that doctrine admits no divergence'.⁷

From the first, Anglican–Roman Catholic discussions of the Doctrine of the Ministry have had to take into account both 'the judgement of the Roman Catholic Church on Anglican Orders'⁸ and the complete absence of any doubt about their orders on the part of Anglicans, as expressed for instance in a letter written in July 1925 by the Archbishop of Canterbury to the Old Catholic Archbishop of Utrecht on the matter.⁹ However, the policy of the Anglican–Roman Catholic Commission has been to approach this question not in isolation but in the context of the *doctrine* of the Church, the sacraments, and the ministry, as was recommended by the Preparatory Commission's 'Malta Report':¹⁰ 'The theology of the ministry forms part of the theology of the Church and must be considered as such. It is only when sufficient agreement has been reached as to the nature of the priesthood and the meaning to be attached in this context to the word "validity" that we could proceed, working always jointly, to the application of this doctrine to the Anglican ministry of today.'

At the first meeting of the International Commission at Windsor in January 1970, Dr Arthur Vogel, in a paper on 'The Church, Intercommunion, and the Ministry', commended the way in which the Anglican–Roman Catholic Consultation in the United States 'tried to avoid hardened attitudes and the mind set of old controversies by looking at the ministry within the setting of the eucharistic community as a whole'. In a parallel paper Fr Jean Tillard asked the primary question: 'Have we the same conception of the nature and purpose of the ministry?', and answered it by showing a remarkable doctrinal convergence in two recent documents: the Ordinal and its Preface drawn up for the proposed Anglican–Methodist Unity Scheme in England, and the Ordination Rites of the new Pontificale Romanum.[11] Following discussion of these and other papers, the Commission was divided into three groups on *Eucharist, Ministry,* and *Authority* to outline the problems and questions to be worked on in preparation for its second full meeting. The group on Ministry proposed that this should be studied under three main headings: The Essence of Ministry, Ministry in a Divided Church, and Renewal and Service. The preparatory work on this was assigned to a subcommission covened by Dr Vogel and Fr Tavard in the United States. They corresponded with Archbishop Arnott, who was a member of the Joint Working Group of the Australian Council of Churches and the Roman Catholic Church which was studying this same subject that year. A position paper on 'Ministry in a Divided Church' was also prepared by Fr Herbert Ryan, SJ.

The International Commission's second meeting took place in Venice in September 1970. The conversations there resulted in the production of three working papers on 'Church and Authority', 'Church and Eucharist', and 'Church and Ministry'. These were published in *Theology, The Clergy Review,* and *One in Christ* in February 1971[12] in order to show the stage the Commission's work had reached and to invite comments and criticisms.

The Venice paper on 'Church and Ministry' spoke first of the Church and the Gospel, and then of the many forms of ministry (*diakonia*), vocation, and the priesthood of Christ which is 'shared in a special way by those who have received holy orders'. The second section of the paper was on 'The Apostolic Ministry'. It affirmed that 'in both our Churches the several orders of [the threefold] ministry are accepted, as sharing, in varying degrees, in the apostolic commission'. Yet differences arise over 'the relation between the episcopate as a whole and the Bishop of Rome'. The third section was on 'The Problem of Orders', and the question was asked 'whether the *new* situation with which we are faced—a pastoral situation—calls for a new policy in the Roman Church'.

At the end of the Venice meeting it was decided that the pattern of the International Commission's future work would be to take one of the three subjects at a time, beginning with the Eucharist. After preparatory work by individuals and by subcommissions in England, South Africa, and North America the third full meeting of the Commission at Windsor in September 1971 completed 'An Agreed Statement on Eucharistic Doctrine', which was published on 31 December that year.[13]

At the conclusion of the meeting at Windsor, plans were made for continuing the International Commission's work on Ministry. Dr Halliburton and Fr Yarnold were asked to convene a subcommission in Oxford to make a study of Ministry in the New Testament. Professor Fairweather and Fr Tillard in Canada examined the concept of 'Sacerdotium'.[14] The Southern African Anglican–Roman Catholic Commission looked at the problem of orders within the general context of Church and Ministry, and use was made of a paper written for that Commission on 'Anglican Orders' by Fr Jerome Smith, OP. Fr George Tavard in the USA was invited to write a paper on 'The Recognition of Ministry'. In addition, full notice was taken of recent studies on the Ministry by individuals and by other dialogue groups. Papers were provided from the Anglican–Roman Catholic Consultation in the USA[15] and from the Joint Working Group of the Australian Council of Churches and the Roman Catholic Church.[16] Special attention was given to the published Report and Papers of the World Council of Churches–Roman Catholic Joint Theological Commission on 'Catholicity and Apostolicity',[17] and to the fourth volume of *Lutherans and Catholics in Dialogue* in the USA on *Eucharist and Ministry*.[18] The relevant section of the Anglican–Lutheran Report[19] was also considered and so was a valuable paper on 'Apostolicity and Ministry' written by Professor R. H. Fuller for the Episcopal–Lutheran Dialogue in the USA in April 1971.[20]

A small subcommission[21] was convened at Woodstock College, New York, in May 1972 by Fr Herbert Ryan to sift and assess all this material, and to suggest an outline way of working. It proposed that the next full meeting of the Commission should examine three subjects: The Church as Eucharistic Community;

Priesthood and Ministry in the New Testament; and A Historical Understanding of the Function of Ministers. Two further subjects were added for a subsequent meeting of the Commission: (*a*) the threefold Order of Ministry, Ordination, and Apostolicity; (*b*) the Church's freedom to alter this pattern, and to recognize ministry and order in itself and in 'separated churches'.

When the full Commission held its fourth meeting at Gazzada near Milan in August–September 1972, the plan of working was changed. This was in response to the need felt to begin not directly with Priesthood but with Mission and the totality of Ministry in the New Testament. It was also agreed not to postpone discussion of Apostolicity. The result of this change of direction was that by the end of the meeting two documents were produced which clarified the Commission's thinking on Ministry in the New Testament and on Apostolicity. The first distinguished between: the unique priesthood of Christ; the priestly ministry exercised by the whole people of God; and the office and function of ministers, which 'originate in the specific purpose of Christ for his Church' and 'are not simply a particular expression of the "priesthood of all believers", but exist to promote the holiness of the whole Church'. The second document spoke of 'the basic apostolicity of the Church', and of apostolicity as 'the quality of all the factors which contribute to the preservation of [the Church's] fidelity' to the apostolic witness to Christ. These two documents formed the basis of the subsequent work of the Commission, but were seen as material to be used as needed rather than as finished sections of a future Statement.

At the end of the Gazzada meeting a provisional structure for a document on Ministry was agreed. Its three main sections were: Apostolic Succession, Priesthood, and Ordination. Subcommissions in Oxford, North America, and Southern Africa were asked to write a draft for each of these, which would be circulated to all members of the Commission for comment. It was arranged that a Subcommittee would meet at Poringland, Norwich, from 11 to 15 June 1973 to take the draft sections and comments and from them to complete a draft document on the Ministry from which the Commission would begin its work at its next full meeting.

In preparation for the Poringland meeting[22] Bishop Clark and Bishop McAdoo each produced a paper incorporating the material received from the Subcommissions, and portions of 'The Ordained Ministry in Ecumenical Perspective' by the World Council of Churches' Faith and Order Commission,[23] the French Roman Catholic–Reformed 'Groupe des Dombes' Statement on the Ministry entitled *Pour une réconciliation des ministères*,[24] and *Lutherans and Catholics in Dialogue* IV.[25] Members of the Subcommittee had also been supplied with a paper by Fr George Tavard, 'A Theological Approach to Ministerial Authority',[26] Bishop Butler's recent articles on the Ministry in *The Tablet*,[27] Bishop Clark's Summary in English of an article by Fr Louis Bouyer, 'Ministère Ecclésiastique et Succession Apostolique',[28] and a passage on the office of bishops from the new *Directorium de Pastorali Ministerio Episcoporum*.[29]

At Poringland it was agreed to start not from the pattern: Christ, the Church, and the Ministry, but from where we are: two churches in which there are ministries and, within these, ordained ministry; to speak next of our role as ministers; and then to give the theological and New Testament justification for this. Discussion focused on the function of *episcope* (oversight) and the role of the ordained minister 'as a unifying figure, as co-ordinator, as judge, as director, as leader who serves'. Ordination as a sacramental act was also debated, and emphasis laid on 2 Cor. 3. 5–6, where St Paul writes that 'our sufficiency is from God'—a reminder of 'the mystery of ministry', and that our faith is 'in the power and authority of Christ in the Spirit in and through the minister'. The Poringland draft document included sections on 'Ministries in the Life of the Church', 'The Co-ordinating Ministry', 'Vocation to the Special Ministry', and 'The Special Minister and the Reconciling Work of Christ'. This last section spoke of the president of the eucharist, ordination in the apostolic succession, and the way priestly terms came to be used of the minister.

The Poringland document was sent to all members of the International Commission for comment and criticism. In preparation for the full meeting at Canterbury from 28 August to 6 September 1973 they also received copies of the Report of the Joint Lutheran–

Roman Catholic Study Commission on 'The Gospel and the Church',[30] the third section of which is on 'The Gospel and the Office of the Ministry in the Church'; the Report of the Joint Commission between the Roman Catholic Church and the World Methodist Council 1967–1970,[31] section 6 of which is on Ministry; the Six Propositions with which the Roman Catholic International Theological Commission concluded their October 1970 Report on *The Priestly Ministry*;[32] and the document on *The Ministerial Priesthood* issued by the Second General Assembly of the Roman Catholic Synod of Bishops in 1971.[33]

The Poringland document was the starting-point for the discussions at Canterbury, which began by considering what should be added to or subtracted from it. The Commission then agreed a draft outline for what was planned to be a biblically and historically informed document on the ministry, which used and applied the material completed at Gazzada and Poringland.

The outline contained an Introduction, followed by sections on Ministries in the Life of the Church (including reference to the New Testament and early Church situation), Ordained Ministry (*episcope*, New Testament images descriptive of the ordained ministry, vocation to holiness, word and sacrament, priesthood and priestly language), Ordination (its unrepeatability, ordination in the apostolic succession), and a Conclusion indicating the import of this agreement in doctrine on the question of the reconciliation of our respective ministries.

This outline was filled out by three drafters, and their draft was then scrutinized, debated, and revised by the full Commission. Out of this process the International Commission's Agreed Statement on the Doctrine of the Ministry emerged. Its conclusion emphasizes that 'agreement on the nature of Ministry is prior to the consideration of the mutual recognition of ministries'. It recognizes 'that we have not yet broached the wide-ranging problems of authority which may arise in any discussion of Ministry, nor the question of primacy'. It considers however 'that our consensus . . . offers a positive contribution to the reconciliation of our churches and of their ministries'.[34]

NOTES

1. Common Declaration of 24 March 1966 in *The Archbishop of Canterbury's Visit to Rome, March 1966* (Church Information Office 1966), p. 14
2. *Anglican-Roman Catholic Dialogue: The Work of the Preparatory Commission*, ed. Alan C. Clark and Colin Davey (Oxford University Press 1974), p. 7. This includes an account of the work of this Commission, its Report and recommendations, and a selection of the papers prepared for it.
3. Anglican-Roman Catholic International Commission, *An Agreed Statement on Eucharistic Doctrine* (SPCK 1972), para. 12. This 'Windsor Statement' was also published in the January 1972 issues of *Theology, The Clergy Review,* and *One in Christ*.
4. *Agreed Statement on Eucharistic Doctrine*, para. 1; *Agreed Statement on the Doctrine of the Ministry*, para. 1 above
5. Para. 17 above
6. Thomas Wieser
7. Para. 17 above
8. Ibid.
9. G. K. A. Bell, *Documents on Christian Unity, a Selection 1920–30* (OUP 1925), p. 202
10. Para. 19: Clark and Davey, op. cit., p. 112
11. J. M. R. Tillard, 'Roman Catholics and Anglicans: the Eucharist', in *One in Christ* (1973 no. 2), pp. 181ff. This is the English translation of a revised and extended version of his original paper which was published in *Nouvelle Revue Théologique*, June 1971.
12. *Theology* (February 1971), pp. 49–67; *The Clergy Review* (February 1971) pp. 126–45; *One in Christ* (nos. 2–3, 1971), pp. 256–76
13. See note 3 above. Commentaries on this have been published by A. M. Allchin, *Eucharist and Unity: Thoughts on the Agreed Statement on Eucharistic Doctrine* (SLG Press, Fairacres, Oxford); Julian Charley, *The Anglican-Roman Catholic Agreement on the Eucharist with an Historical Introduction and Theological Commentary* (Grove Books, Bramcote, Notts); Bishop Alan C. Clark, *Agreement on the Eucharist: the Windsor Statement with an Introduction and Commentary* (RC Ecumenical Commission of England and Wales, 44 Gray's Inn Road, London WC1); Fr Herbert Ryan, SJ, in *Worship*, January 1972, pp. 6–14. For the background papers to the Windsor Agreed Statement and a brief bibliography, see *One in Christ*, 1973 no. 2, pp. 106–98, and *Lumen Vitae*, Brussels, 1973 no. 1, pp. 113–75. The Statement is also included in *Modern Eucharistic Agreement* (SPCK 1973), which has a Foreword by Bishop Alan C. Clark and an Introductory Essay by Bishop H. R. McAdoo.

14. Fr Tillard's paper on 'The "Sacerdotal" Quality of the Christian Ministry' has now been published under the title *What Priesthood has the Ministry?* as no. 13 of Grove Booklets on Ministry and Worship, Grove Books, Bramcote, Notts, and in the 1973 no. 3 issue of *One in Christ*, pp. 237-69.
15. Including 'The Function of the Minister in the Eucharistic Celebration: An Ecumenical Approach', by Fr George Tavard, published in the *Journal of Ecumenical Studies*, vol. 4, no. 4, 1967
16. *Ministry*, the Report and Papers from its fourth meeting in Sydney, May 1970, was produced by the Australian Council of Churches, Third Floor, 511 Kent Street, Sydney, NSW 2000
17. Published in the 1970 no. 3 issue of *One in Christ*
18. Published 1970 by Representatives of the USA National Committee of the Lutheran World Federation (315 Park Avenue South, New York 10010) and the Bishops' Committee for Ecumenical and Interreligious Affairs (Publications Office, US Catholic Conference, 1312 Massachusetts Avenue NW, Washington, DC 20005)
19. *Anglican-Lutheran International Conversations* (SPCK 1973) and pp. 139-75 of *Lutheran-Episcopal Dialogue, A Progress Report* (Forward Movement Maxi Book, USA 1972)
20. Published in *Concordia Theological Monthly* February 1972, and in *Lutheran-Episcopal Dialogue, A Progress Report*, pp. 76-93, under the title The Development of the Ministry
21. Its members were: Bishop Clark, Bishop McAdoo, Bishop Vogel, Fr Tillard, Fr Tavard, Prof. Fairweather, Mr Charley, and Fr John Reid, SJ.
22. Those present were Bishop Clark, Bishop McAdoo, Bishop Butler, Bishop Moorman, Fr Tillard, Fr Duprey, Mr Charley, and Mr Davey.
23. Published as item SE/34 in *Study Encounter*, vol. viii, no. 4, obtainable from the Publications Office, WCC, 150 route de Ferney, CH-1211, Geneva 20, Switzerland [A revised version appears on pp. 111-141 below]
24. Published by Les Presses de Taizé, F-71460, Taizé, France, January 1973 [pp. 89-107 below]
25. See note 18 above.
26. Printed in *The Jurist*, vol. 32, no. 3, Summer 1972, pp. 311-29, published by the School of Canon Law, the Catholic University of America, Washington, DC.
27. *The Tablet*, 17 and 24 February and 3 March 1973
28. Published in *Nouvelle Revue Théologique*, March 1973, pp. 251-2
29. Vatican 1973, paras. 13-26
30. Published in *Lutheran World*, vol. 19, no. 3, 1972

31. Published in the Information Service of the Secretariat for Promoting Christian Unity, no. 21, May 1973/III, pp. 22–38
32. Published by Editions du Cerf, 29 Boulevard Latour-Maubourg, Paris VIII
33. Published by the Vatican Polyglot Press, 1971
34. Para. 17 above

MEMBERS OF THE COMMISSION

ANGLICAN DELEGATES

The Rt Revd H. R. McAdoo, Bishop of Ossory, Ferns and Leighlin (Co-Chairman)

The Most Revd F. R. Arnott, Archbishop of Brisbane

The Rt Revd J. R. H. Moorman, Bishop of Ripon

The Rt Revd E. G. Knapp-Fisher, Bishop of Pretoria

The Rt Revd A. A. Vogel, Bishop of West Missouri

The Very Revd Henry Chadwick, Dean of Christ Church, Oxford

The Revd J. W. Charley, Vice-Principal, St John's College, Nottingham

The Revd Dr Eugene Fairweather, Keble Professor of Divinity, Trinity College, University of Toronto

The Revd Canon H. E. Root, Professor of Theology, University of Southampton

CONSULTANT

The Revd Dr R. J. Halliburton, Vice-Principal, St Stephen's House, Oxford

SECRETARY

The Revd Colin Davey, Assistant Chaplain, Archbishop of Canterbury's Counsellors on Foreign Relations

ROMAN CATHOLIC DELEGATES

The Rt Revd Alan C. Clark, Auxiliary Bishop of Northampton (Co-Chairman)

The Rt Revd Christopher Butler, OSB, Auxiliary Bishop of Westminster

The Revd Fr Barnabas Ahern, CP, Professor of Sacred Scripture, Rome

The Revd Fr P. Duprey, WF, Under Secretary, Vatican Secretariat for Promoting Christian Unity

The Revd Fr Herbert Ryan, SJ, Professor of Historical Theology, Pontifical Faculty of Theology, Woodstock College, New York

Professor J. J. Scarisbrick, Professor of History, University of Warwick

The Revd Fr George Tavard, AA, Professor of Theology, Methodist Theological School, Delaware, Ohio

The Revd Fr Jean M. R. Tillard, OP, Professor of Dogmatic Theology in the Dominican Faculty of Theology (Ottawa) and in Brussels

The Revd Fr E. J. Yarnold, SJ, Senior Tutor, Campion Hall, Oxford

SECRETARY

The Rt Revd Mgr W. A. Purdy, Staff Member, Vatican Secretariat for Promoting Christian Unity

WORLD COUNCIL OF CHURCHES OBSERVER

The Revd Dr Gunther Gassmann, Research Professor, Centre d'Etudes Oecuméniques, Strasbourg

THE STATUS OF THE DOCUMENT

The document published here is the work of the Anglican–Roman Catholic International Commission.

As the two Co-Chairmen point out in their Preface, it is at present no more than a joint statement of the Commission. The Commission is reporting to the authorities who appointed it on one of the items in its programme of work. These authorities have allowed the Statement to be published so that it may be discussed by other theologians. It is not a declaration by the Roman Catholic Church or by the Anglican Communion. It does not authorize any change in existing ecclesiastical discipline.

The Commission will be glad to receive observations and criticisms made in a constructive and fraternal spirit. Its work is done in the service of the Church. It will give responsible attention to every serious comment which is likely to help in improving or completing the result so far achieved. This wider collaboration will make its work to a greater degree work in common, and by God's grace will lead us to the goal set at the beginning of Anglican–Roman Catholic dialogue: 'that unity in truth for which Christ prayed' (Common Declaration of Pope Paul VI and the Archbishop of Canterbury, March 1966).

Comments on the Statement or requests for further information on the work of the Commission may be sent to its Secretaries:

The Reverend Colin Davey, The Archbishop of Canterbury's Counsellors on Foreign Relations, Palace Court, 222 Lambeth Road, London SE1 7LB (Tel: 01-928 4880).

The Rt Reverend Mgr William Purdy, Vatican Secretariat for Promoting Christian Unity, Vatican City, 00193, Rome, Italy (Tel: Rome 698-4533).

EUCHARIST AND MINISTRY

A Lutheran–Roman Catholic Statement

ST LOUIS, MISSOURI 1970

Extracted from *Lutherans and Catholics in Dialogue*

Eucharist and Ministry

Published jointly by Representatives of the
USA National Committee of the Lutheran World Federation
and the Bishops' Committee for Ecumenical and
Interreligious Affairs 1970

© The Publishers 1970

FOREWORD

This volume is the fourth in a series designed to share with interested clergy and laity the progress made in the course of theological conversations between representatives of the Lutheran and the Roman Catholic traditions. The first volume, published in 1965, dealt with the subject 'The Status of the Nicene Creed as Dogma of the Church'. The second series of conversations dealt with the topic 'One Baptism for the Remission of Sins'. In both of these areas of theological concern the participants from the two communions found themselves in general agreement, a fact which they had anticipated but which added substantially to mutual understanding regarding the ways according to which each group proceeds theologically, and also indicated to some extent that consideration of future scheduled topics would require intensified research within the perspective of the astonishing ecclesiastical developments of the last decade.

Therefore it came as no surprise that the discussions on 'The Eucharist as Sacrifice', a controversial issue which has estranged Lutherans from Roman Catholics for four centuries, required a much longer period of dialogue and uncovered more knotty problems than could be solved in that series of conversations. Nevertheless, the joint statement approved unanimously by participants on both sides represented a remarkable advance in convergence toward a common understanding on this critical theological point, something for which we can only acknowledge with humility and thanks the effective working of the Holy Spirit among us.

It seemed natural to take up as the next point the question of intercommunion. A week-end of conversations on this subject quickly revealed that one could not even discuss the matter without considering the key question of a valid Ministry in relation to the administration of the eucharist. Therefore the question of intercommunion was set aside until the groups could concentrate on the subject 'Eucharist and Ministry'. Over two years was spent in the preparation of studies, in conversations and drafting, the results of which are reflected in this volume. Again, while some points of importance remain unresolved, the common statement of the group, adopted unanimously, together with the separate statements of the representatives of the two traditions represent a forward step of immense significance. Those who have participated in this series of conversations again bear testimony to their awareness of the workings of the Holy Spirit in their midst and trust that the readers of this volume will find it as stimulating and instructive in the furthering of their concerns toward Christian unity as did those who are responsible for the studies and statements which are here reported.

It must again be emphasized that the studies and position papers contained herein represent the views of the authors and of the dialogue groups, and do not constitute official statements by any of the churches of which they are members.

It is anticipated that the dialogues will continue with the consideration of at least two or three additional theological issues which have been stumbling-blocks to mutual understanding between Lutherans and Roman Catholics in the past. We hope fervently that these efforts will make at least a modest contribution toward the ultimate outward realization of the oneness which all Christians have in Jesus Christ.

PAUL C. EMPIE
✠ T. AUSTIN MURPHY

Part One
COMMON OBSERVATIONS ON EUCHARISTIC MINISTRY

INTRODUCTION

1. The problem of the Ministry[1] is an inevitable item on any agenda of doctrinal discussion between Roman Catholics and Lutherans. In each of our other discussions, we have found ourselves confronted by it.

2. In our treatment of the Nicene Creed and the significance of dogmatic statements we saw the necessary connection between dogma (i.e. authoritative creeds and confessions) and the teaching authority of the Church.[2] Our dialogue on baptism made it possible for us to confess together our faith that this sacrament is an act of Christ by which God calls his Church into being. At the same time we recognized that differences of interpretation of this sacramental act have frequently been rooted in differing understandings of the ministry of the Church.[3]

3. Sessions devoted to the problems of the eucharist as sacrifice and of the presence of Christ in the sacrament showed again a remarkable agreement in these much controverted topics, but also showed us how many matters could be cleared up only by discussion of the question of the minister of the eucharist.[4] This became even more clear when we devoted one meeting to the problems of receiving communion in each other's eucharistic celebrations. There we recognized that a solution was not possible until the problems of the Ministry were squarely faced.

4. In our sessions dealing with the ministry, as in our other discussions, we have attempted to clear away misunderstandings, to clarify to each other the theological concerns of our traditions, and to see what common affirmations we can make about the reality of

the Ministry. Neither Catholic nor Lutheran participants came to this dialogue with a complete doctrine of this ministry and we have not formulated one in our discussions. We have found certain areas that we judge are central to this reality and critical for the unity of the Church. In these areas we make common affirmations. We gratefully acknowledge the contribution of the ongoing discussion of the Ministry in the Ecumenical Movement, both for its clarification of the theological issues and for its service in prodding us to do our thinking about the Ministry in a responsibly ecumenical context.[5]

5. Again we have noted that in our use of the same terms, we have not always meant the same things, and that differing theological language has sometimes masked theological concerns which are similar if not identical. We are convinced that in spite of differing vocabularies and problematics we are both approaching greater agreement on what God is doing in his Church, as is evidenced in the following paragraphs.

I

THE MINISTRY IN THE CONTEXT OF GOD'S ACT IN CHRIST

6. Both the Catholic and the Lutheran traditions confess that God fulfils his promise to his people and definitively reveals his saving love for the world in the life, death, resurrection, and coming again of Jesus Christ. The God of Israel acts and speaks in the deeds and words of his Son.

7. Scripture attests that it was through the work of the Holy Spirit that Jews and Gentiles alike repented, believed, and were baptized. Thus were men united by Christ into the unique community called the Church.

8. The Lord of the Church, through the Holy Spirit, continues to act sacramentally and to proclaim his teaching through the men whom he has united with himself. The words and acts of Jesus in which the God of Israel has revealed his love for all mankind are the 'good news'. Under the guidance of the Spirit the first

believers proclaimed by deed and word this gospel of the saving presence, activity, and teaching of the Lord.

9. The Church has, then, the task of proclaiming the gospel to all, believers and unbelievers. This task or service of the whole Church is spoken of as 'ministry' (*diakonia*). In the course of this statement, we employ the term ministry (lower case *m*, with or without the definite article) in this sense. The ministry of the Church, thus defined, will be distinguished from the (or a) Ministry, a particular form of service—a specific order, function or gift (charism) within and for the sake of Christ's Church in its mission to the world. The term Minister in this document refers to the person to whom this Ministry has been entrusted. We are convinced that the special Ministry must not be discussed in isolation but in the context of the ministry of the whole people of God.

II
THE MINISTRY IN THE CONTEXT OF THE CHURCH

A. THE MINISTRY OF THE PEOPLE OF GOD

10. The ministry which devolves upon the whole Church can rightly be described as a priestly service (*hierateuma*, cf. 1 Pet. 2. 5, 9), such as that of ancient Israel, whom Yahweh fashioned into 'a kingdom of priests and a holy nation' among all peoples (Exod. 19. 5–6). We are agreed that in Jesus Christ God has provided his people with a high priest and sacrifice (cf. Heb. 4. 14ff). All who are united with Jesus as Christ and Lord by baptism and faith are also united with, and share, his priesthood. We recognize therefore that the whole Church has a priesthood in Christ, i.e. a ministry or service from God to men, that 'they may see your good deeds and glorify God on the day of visitation' (1 Pet. 2. 12). They are thus privileged and obliged to represent the concerns of God to men and those of men to God.

11. To enable the Church to be what God intends it to be in and for the world, God bestows within this priesthood various gifts for ministering. In particular, 'God has appointed . . . apostles,

prophets, teachers', etc. (1 Cor. 12. 28–30; cf. Rom. 12. 6–8; Eph. 4. 7–12). While no single Ministry mentioned in the New Testament corresponds exactly to the special Ministry of the later Church,[6] many of the specialized tasks of which we hear in the New Testament are entrusted to that later Ministry: preaching the gospel, administering what the Church came to call sacraments, caring for the faithful. We turn now to what we can say in common of this special Ministry in the Church (keeping in mind the particular aspect of our study—valid Ministry in relation to the eucharist).

B. THE SPECIAL MINISTRY

12. Just as the Church is to be seen in the light of God's love, his act in Christ, and the work of the Spirit, so also the Ministry is to be seen in the light of the love of God, his saving act in Jesus Christ, and the ongoing activity of the Holy Spirit. This Ministry has the twofold task of proclaiming the gospel to the world—evangelizing, witnessing, serving—and of building up in Christ those who already believe—teaching, exhorting, reproving, and sanctifying, by word and sacrament. For this twofold work, the Spirit endows the Ministry with varieties of gifts, and thus helps the Church to meet new situations in its pilgrimage. Through proclamation of the word and administration of the sacraments, this Ministry serves to unify and order the Church in a special way for its ministry.[7]

13. The Ministry stands with the people of God under Christ but also speaks in the name of Christ to his people. On the one hand, the Ministry as part of the Church's ministry stands under the Word and the Spirit, under judgement as well as under grace. But it also has a special role within the ministry of the people of God, proclaiming God's Word, administering the sacraments, exhorting and reproving.[8]

14. This Ministry is 'apostolic'. The term 'apostolic' has had a variety of references: it has been applied for instance to doctrine, practices, authority.[9] Indeed, the *variety* of ways in which the gospel is expressed in the early Church may be recognized as a feature of apostolicity.[10]

15. Apostolicity has usually implied some sort of succession in what is apostolic. For many Catholics the phrase 'apostolic succession' has meant succession in the ministerial office as a sign of unbroken transmission from the apostles. The stress for Lutherans has been on succession in apostolic doctrine. Historical studies have shown that in the New Testament and patristic periods there was stress on doctrinal succession; there also arose an emphasis on succession in apostolic office as a very important way of ensuring doctrinal succession and thus providing a sign of unity and a defence against heresy.[11]

16. Entry into the Ministry has been designated by both Catholics and Lutherans as 'ordination'. This term too has had a variety of meanings. Catholics have seen in ordination a sacramental act, involving a gift of the Holy Spirit, a charism for the service of the Church and the world, the designation to a special service in the Church, and the quality of permanence and unrepeatability. Lutherans, using a different (and more restricted) definition of sacrament, have generally been reluctant to use 'sacrament' with reference to ordination, although the *Apology* of the Augsburg Confession is willing to do so (13, 9–13). Because of post-Reformation polemics, Lutherans became even more reluctant to use the term. Their consistent practice, however, shows a conviction concerning the sacramental reality of ordination to the Ministry. Lutherans too invoke the Holy Spirit for the gifts of the Ministry, see ordination as the setting apart for a specific service in the Church and for the world, and regard the act as having a once-for-all significance.[12] Thus there is considerable convergence between the Catholic and the Lutheran understandings of ordination.

17. The expressions 'character' and 'indelible' have been used by Catholics with reference to ordination to describe the aspects of gift, charism, designation, and the qualities of permanence and unrepeatability.[13] Lutherans have objected to these terms because of the metaphysical implications they understand to be involved in them. However, historical studies and the renewal of liturgical and sacramental theology have brought into our discussions an emphasis upon the functional aspect of character and upon the

gift of the Spirit.[14] These factors may help us to overcome traditional disagreements and open the way to a common approach to this complex of problems.

18. Having discussed the terms 'apostolic', 'ordination', and 'character', we now affirm together that entry into this apostolic and God-given Ministry is by ordination. No man ordains himself or can claim this office as his right, but he is called by God and designated in and through the Church. In reference to what has been called 'character', we are agreed that ordination to the Ministry is for a lifetime of service and is not to be repeated.

C. THE STRUCTURING OF THE SPECIAL MINISTRY

19. Although we agree that Christ has given his Church a special order of Ministry, we must also acknowledge the diverse ways in which this Ministry has been structured and implemented in the Catholic and Lutheran traditions.

20. In Catholicism, the Ministry of order has been apportioned among three Ministries or major orders: deacon, priest (*presbyter*), and bishop. All are conferred by a rite of ordination that includes the laying on of hands. The distribution of ministerial functions among these orders varies and has varied. In the present discipline, all three are appointed to baptize and proclaim the gospel; only priests and bishops celebrate the eucharist; only bishops ordain to major orders. Without prejudice to their belief that it is the bishop who possesses the fulness of the Ministry conferred by ordination,[15] Catholics note that it is both historically and theologically significant that priests have ordained others as priests.[16]

21. The Lutheran tradition has one order of ordained Ministers, usually called pastors, which combines features of the episcopate and the presbyterate. This Ministry is also conferred by a rite of ordination that includes the laying on of hands. The pastor who has received this Ministry possesses the fulness of that which ordination confers and in general he corresponds in his functions with the bishop in the Catholic tradition.[17] In the Lutheran Churches represented in this dialogue, the ordination of pastors

is reserved to the district or synodical president or a pastor designated by him. The ordination of pastors in these Churches goes back historically to priests ordained in the Catholic tradition who, on becoming Lutherans and lacking Catholic bishops who would impose hands on successors, themselves imposed hands for the ordination of co-workers and successors in the Ministry. From the Lutheran standpoint, such an ordination in presbyterial succession designates and qualifies the Lutheran pastor for all the functions that the Catholic priest (*presbyter*) exercises, including that of celebrating a eucharist which would be called (in Catholic terminology) valid. It is to be noted, however, that the Lutheran confessions indicate a preference for retaining the traditional episcopal order and discipline of the Church, and express regret that no bishop was willing to ordain priests for evangelical congregations.[18]

22. These ways in which the Ministry has been structured and implemented in our two traditions appear to us to be consonant with apostolic teaching and practice. We are agreed that the basic reality of the apostolic Ministry can be preserved amid variations in structure and implementation, in rites of ordination and in theological explanation. As we learn more of the complex history of the Ministry, we begin to grasp the ways in which this gift of God to his Church is able to assimilate valuable elements from different ages and cultures without losing its authentic apostolic character. In this context we find that the present moment speaks persuasively to us, urging both the renewal of what is basic in our apostolic heritage as well as openness to the variants that our Christian witness to the world requires. In presenting these common observations on the eucharistic Ministry we are aware of the difficulties implied therein for both of our traditions,[19] as our respective reflections in the following two chapters indicate. That we have not found these difficulties insuperable is indicated by the recommendations which each group has been able to make. We rejoice together at the future prospect of Christian recognition and reconciliation opened by these recommendations.

Part Two
REFLECTIONS OF THE LUTHERAN PARTICIPANTS

23. Lutherans approach the questions dealt with in this common statement on the basis of the conviction that their churches belong to the one, holy, catholic, and apostolic Church. They regard their ordained clergymen as persons validly set apart for the Ministry of the gospel and of the sacraments in the Church of Christ. They hold that the sacraments that these ordained clergymen administer in their midst are valid sacraments. In their confessional writings, the Lutherans claim to stand in the authentic Catholic tradition.[1]

24. On the basis of their confessional writings, Lutherans also affirm the churchly character of the Roman Catholic community and the validity of the Roman Catholic Church's Ministry and sacraments. For Lutherans the Church exists wherever there is a community of believers among whom the gospel of God's grace in Christ is responsibly proclaimed and applied and the sacraments are administered in accordance with our Lord's intention.[2] The responsible proclaiming and applying of the gospel and the administering of the sacraments require that persons be set aside for this office and function.[3]

25. Some Lutherans have had misgivings in the area of Roman Catholic commitment to the gospel. Nevertheless, Lutherans have always held that as long as the gospel is proclaimed in any Christian community in such a way that it remains the gospel and as long as the sacraments are administered in that community in such a way that they are channels of the Holy Spirit, human beings are through these means reborn to everlasting life and the Church continues to subsist in these communities. We believe that the Roman Catholic Church meets these criteria.

26. Noteworthy in this connection is the insistence of the Lutheran

symbolical books that the Church never ceased to exist down to their own time. Concretely they declare that St Bernard of Clairvaux (1090–1153), the most famous son of the Cistercian Order, St Dominic Guzman (1170–1221), founder of the Order of Preachers, and St Francis of Assisi (1181?–1226), founder of the Order of Friars Minor, are 'holy fathers' (*sancti patres*).[4] As evidence of the persistence of the Church and of the communication of the Holy Spirit within it through baptism, the *Book of Concord* cites not only St Bernard, but also, bracketed with him, two late medieval churchmen of quite diverse theological views, John le Charlier de Gerson (1363–1429) of the university of Paris and John Uus (1369?–1415) of Prague.[5]

27. There is no doubt in Lutheran minds that the Roman Catholic Church subscribes to the fundamental Trinitarian and Christological dogmas, 'the high articles of the divine majesty' (Smalcald Articles, Part One). Lutherans must take seriously the Roman Catholic Church's profession of the Catholic creeds—including the 'for us men and for our salvation' and the 'was crucified also for us' of the creed of Constantinople ('Nicene Creed') and the 'suffered for our salvation' of the Symbol *Quicunque vult* ('Athanasian Creed'). The Roman Catholic Church affirms its kinship with 'those Christians who openly confess Jesus Christ as God and Lord and as the sole Mediator between God and man to the glory of one God, Father, Son, and Holy Spirit.'[6] Lutherans are well aware that Roman Catholics pray the same Sunday collects that Lutherans pray (including those that stress man's helplessness and salvation by grace alone, such as those for Sexagesima Sunday, the Second Sunday in Lent, Laetare Sunday, Easter Day, and the First, Third, Eighth, Twelfth, Fourteenth, Sixteenth, and Eighteenth Sundays after Trinity). They know too that the Roman Catholic Church affirms the gospel in unmistakable terms in many other places of its liturgy—for example, the *Exultet* in the Easter Eve office and the *Veni, Sancte Spiritus*, in Whitsuntide.[7]

28. The episcopal structure and polity of the Roman Catholic Church does not in itself constitute a problem for Lutherans. Indeed, the *Book of Concord* itself affirms the desire of the

Lutheran reformers to preserve, if possible, the episcopal polity that they had inherited from the past.[8] As long as the ordained Ministry is retained, any form of polity which serves the proclamation of the gospel is acceptable. Within their own community some Lutherans have episcopacy with a formal 'apostolic succession'[9] (e.g. Sweden, Finland, and some Asian and African churches). Other Lutherans have episcopacy without the 'apostolic succession' (e.g. Norway, Denmark, Iceland, and Germany). Lutherans also have or have had churches governed by synods, by consistories, and by ministeria.

29. Even with the misgivings that sixteenth-century Lutherans had about the papacy,[10] the Lutheran symbolical books recognize the bishop of Rome as the lawful pastor of the church in that city.[11] In fact, the confessional writings do not exclude the possibility that the papacy might have a symbolic or functional value in a wider area as long as its primacy is seen as being of human right.[12]

30. We have no basis in the *Book of Concord* for denying that Roman Catholic priests are competent Ministers of the gospel and the sacraments. While some Lutherans in times past have doubted that the Ministry of Roman Catholic clergymen is really a Ministry of the gospel, the fact that Vatican II has called the proclamation of the gospel of God to all a 'primary duty' of priests in the Roman Catholic church[13] should remove these uncertainties.

31. Within this context, we see no reason for doubting the validity of the sacrament of the altar within the Roman Catholic Church.[14] In conformity with the Lutheran confessional writings, we hold that the distribution and reception of the sacrament in one kind only, conflicts with the biblical injunction, but we do not hold that this invalidates the sacrament that Roman Catholic communicants receive. We note that Eastern Catholics in union with Rome have always received holy communion under both kinds. We likewise observe with joy the increasing frequency with which members of Roman-rite congregations are communicated under both kinds in the Roman Catholic Church since Vatican II.

32. There are Lutherans who do not find it easy to overcome

their concerns about the inferences that they have heard drawn from the Roman Catholic teaching of transubstantiation, about some of the language in which the sacrificial aspect of the sacrament of the altar has been popularly described, and about some of the attitudes and practices involving the reserved sacrament. But we observe that, in terms of the Lutheran theology of consecration, these things do not affect the *validity* of the sacrament of the altar as Roman Catholic priests celebrate and dispense it. At the same time, we have taken cognizance elsewhere of the official Roman Catholic instruction on eucharistic worship (1967) which asserts that the 'primary and original purpose of the reservation of the sacrament is the communication of the sick' and that 'the adoration of Christ present in the reserved sacrament is of later origin and is a secondary end'.[15] In the same connection we have gratefully recorded the increasing measure of agreement between Lutherans and Roman Catholics on the sacrificial aspects of the sacrament of the altar. We have likewise stated that today 'when Lutheran theologians read contemporary (Roman) Catholic expositions, it becomes clear to them that the dogma of transubstantiation intends to affirm the fact of Christ's presence and of the change which takes place and is not an attempt to explain how Christ becomes present'.[16]

33. Although we see our common statement as removing some of the obstacles that separate Roman Catholics and Lutherans, there are still problems to be discussed before we can recommend pulpit and altar fellowship. The common statement that precedes these reflections does not provide an adequate basis for the establishment of such fellowship. Nor does it constitute approval by either community of every practice fostered or tolerated by the other community.

34. We Lutherans are conscious of the real and imagined differences that centuries of mutual separation have built up between us and Roman Catholics. We are sensitive to the canonical, traditional, and psychological barriers to eucharistic sharing that are present in both communities. We are aware of the many doctrinal discussions with other churches that both the Roman Catholic and the Lutheran Churches in the United States are

conducting, and recognize the magnitude of the theological work that still needs to be done.[17]

35. *As Lutherans, we joyfully witness that in theological dialogue with our Roman Catholic partners we have again seen clearly a fidelity to the proclamation of the gospel and the administration of the sacraments which confirms our historic conviction that the Roman Catholic Church is an authentic church of our Lord Jesus Christ. For this reason we recommend to those who have appointed us that through appropriate channels the participating Lutheran churches be urged to declare formally their judgement that the ordained Ministers of the Roman Catholic Church are engaged in a valid Ministry of the gospel, announcing the gospel of Christ and administering the sacraments of faith[18] as their chief responsibilities, and that the body and blood of our Lord Jesus Christ are truly present in their celebrations of the sacrament of the altar.*

Part Three
REFLECTIONS OF THE ROMAN CATHOLIC PARTICIPANTS

INTRODUCTION

36. At first glance the Roman Catholic attitude toward the Lutheran eucharistic Ministry would seem easily determinable. A simplified expression of the traditional Roman Catholic outlook is that those who preside at the eucharist do so in virtue of being ordained by a bishop who stands in succession to the apostles who received from Christ the commission, 'Do this in commemoration of me'. Without such ordination a man can make no claim to a valid eucharistic Ministry. Now, at the time of the Reformation in Germany the bishops did not ordain Ministers for the congregations that professed to follow Martin Luther; and so it came about that priests who had adopted Lutheran beliefs ordained other men to preside at the eucharist,[1] thus perpetuating a presbyteral rather than an episcopal succession. Among most Lutherans there is no claim to an episcopate in historical succession to the apostles.[2] Thus the Lutheran eucharistic Ministry would seem to be deficient in what Catholics have hitherto regarded as essential elements.

37. Yet, as we Catholics in this dialogue have examined the problem, our traditional objections to the Lutheran eucharistic Ministry were seen to be of less force today, and reasons emerged for a positive reappraisal. We may group our reflections below under the headings of historical arguments and theological arguments.

I
HISTORICAL ARGUMENTS

38. It is impossible to prove from the New Testament that the only Ministers of the eucharist were the apostles, their appointed successors, and those ordained by their successors. Modern biblical investigations have shown that there were several different concepts of 'apostle' in the New Testament.[3] While Luke-Acts is representative of a strain of New Testament thought that would equate the apostles with the Twelve and hence with those whom Jesus commanded, 'Do this in commemoration of me', Paul is representative of a wider (and perhaps earlier) view whereby men like himself could be apostles even though they had not been disciples of Jesus during his lifetime. There is no clear biblical evidence that the Twelve were the exclusive Ministers of the eucharist in New Testament times or that they appointed men to preside at the eucharist. (On the other hand, we may add that neither is there evidence that all Christians were eligible Ministers of the eucharist.) While in the local churches, founded by apostles like Paul, there were leaders or persons in authority, we are told very little about how such men were appointed and nothing about their presiding at the eucharist. Even in the Pastoral Epistles (which are of uncertain date), in which there is described a church order featuring bishop-presbyters, we are not told that such figures had a eucharistic Ministry. Of course, this argument drawn from the silence of the New Testament has serious limitations, and the eucharistic practice may have been far more definite than the limited evidence proves. We must insist, however, in face of this silence, how difficult it is to make affirmations about what is necessary in the eucharistic Ministry.

39. At the beginning of the second century (but perhaps even earlier), as attested by Ignatius of Antioch, the bishop had emerged as the highest authority in the local church, and either he or his appointee presided at the eucharist. However, we are not certain how the Ignatian bishop was appointed or that he stood in a chain of historical succession to the apostles by means of

ordination or even that the pattern described by Ignatius was universal in the church. Some find in Didache 10. 7 evidence that wandering charismatic prophets could preside at the eucharist.[4]

40. When the episcopate and the presbyterate had become a general pattern in the Church, the historical picture still presents uncertainties that affect judgement on the Minister of the eucharist. For instance, is the difference between a bishop and a priest of divine ordination? St Jerome maintained that it was not;[5] and the Council of Trent, wishing to respect Jerome's opinion, did not undertake to define that the pre-eminence of the bishop over presbyters was by divine law.[6] If the difference is not of divine ordination, the reservation to the bishop of the power of ordaining Ministers of the eucharist would be a church decision. In fact, in the history of the Church there are instances of priests (i.e. presbyters) ordaining other priests, and there is evidence that the church accepted and recognized the Ministry of priests so ordained.[7]

41. By way of summation, we find from the historical evidence that by the sixteenth century there had been a long and almost exclusive practice whereby the only Minister of the eucharist was one ordained by a bishop who had been consecrated as heir to a chain of episcopal predecessors. Yet, in this long history there are lacunae, along with exceptions that offer some precedent for the practice adopted by the Lutherans.

II

THEOLOGICAL ARGUMENTS

42. The negative appraisal of the Lutheran eucharistic Ministry that has been traditional among Catholics was not based solely or even chiefly on an analysis of the historical evidence favouring episcopal ordination. Theological factors entered prominently into this appraisal. Here again, however, as we Catholic participants in the dialogue examined the difficulties, we found that they no longer seemed insuperable.

43. A. The question of an authentic eucharistic Ministry in a worshipping community is intimately related to an evaluation of that community as part of the Church. The unity that is signified and realized by the reception of the eucharistic body of Christ is related to the unity of the body of Christ which is the Church. Formerly the Roman Catholic Church did not speak of the Christian denominations that resulted from the Reformation as churches; but in the Second Vatican Council these groups were spoken of as 'churches or ecclesial communities',[8] a change that seems to have theological implications.[9] Not all Catholic theologians would conclude that because a Christian community possesses 'ecclesial reality', its table fellowship is necessarily graced by the presence of the body and blood of the Lord. Nevertheless, our ability to recognize the Lutheran communities as churches removes a barrier to our favourable understanding of the Lutheran sacred Ministry. We are now obliged to reassess whether the Lutheran communities may not be churches that truly celebrate the holy eucharist.[10]

44. B. It may be objected that while the Lutheran communities do constitute churches, they are defective churches in an essential note that has ramifications for the eucharistic Ministry, namely, apostolicity. This charge is true if apostolicity is defined so as necessarily to include apostolic succession through episcopal consecration.[11] However, it is dubious that apostolicity should be so defined. In the first two centuries of Christianity, apostolic succession in doctrine (fidelity to the gospel) was considered more important than simple succession in office or orders.[12] The lists of bishops that appeared late in the second century were intended to demonstrate more a line of legitimatized teachers than a line of sacramental validity.[13] Undoubtedly apostolic succession through episcopal consecration is a valuable sign and aspect of apostolicity, for in church history there is a mutual interplay between doctrinal integrity and the succession of those who are its official teachers. Yet, despite the lack of episcopal succession, the Lutheran church by its devotion to gospel, creed, and sacrament has preserved a form of doctrinal apostolicity.[14]

45. C. In the past, Catholics commonly assumed that Lutherans did not believe in the real presence of Christ's body and blood, sacramentally offered in the eucharistic sacrifice, and consequently were presumably not ordaining a eucharistic Ministry in the sense in which Catholics understood eucharist. This assumption of defective intent now appears to us unfounded; for in our joint statement on the eucharist, we Catholics and Lutherans affirmed our agreement on the real presence and on the sacrificial character of the Lord's supper.[15]

46. D. Still another Catholic difficulty about the Lutheran eucharistic Ministry arose from a fear that the Lutheran understanding of the sacred Ministry was defective. In examining a number of points discussed below, we found that, while there are differences of emphasis and phrasing in the theologies of our respective churches, there is also a gratifying degree of agreement as to the essentials of the sacred Ministry.

47. 1) Do Lutherans recognize that the Sacred Ministry is of divine institution? We find the Lutheran affirmation, 'God instituted the sacred Ministry of teaching the gospel and administering the sacraments'.[16] Also, 'The Church institutes clergymen by divine command', so that 'ordination performed by a pastor in his own church is valid by divine right'.[17]

48. 2) Do Lutherans conceive of the sacred Ministry as simply or primarily a Ministry of the word (preaching) rather than of sacrament? We have found a frequent joining of word and sacrament in the Lutheran writings on the subject. It is true that in the sixteenth century the Lutherans gave emphasis to a Ministry of the word in reaction to what they saw as a danger of a purely ritualistic Ministry. In response, Catholics tended to give emphasis to the dispensation of the sacraments, lest the importance of that factor in Ministry be denigrated. In the less apologetic atmosphere currently prevailing, both groups see that the task of the Ministry includes both word and sacrament.

49. 3) Do Lutherans see the sacred Ministry as something beyond or distinct from the general ministry of all believers? It is quite clear that the Lutherans have a concept of a *special* Ministry in

the church. 'The symbolical books see the sacred ministry both as an office (*ministerium; Amt*) and as an order or estate (*ordo; Stand*) within the church.'[18] There have been disagreements among Lutheran theologians about the relation of the special Ministry to the universal priesthood of believers.[19] Catholic theologians too have been unable to state this relationship with complete accord; yet we do find the statement made by the Second Vatican Council that the common priesthood of the faithful and the ministerial priesthood differ from one another in essence and not only in degree.[20] On the Lutheran side there is the affirmation: 'We say that no one should be allowed to administer the word and the sacraments in the Church unless he is duly called'.[21] Theologians of both churches need to clarify further the relation between clergy and laity and to analyse the biblical concept of the royal priesthood of God's people in order to see if that concept really tells us anything about eucharistic Ministry.[22]

50. 4) Do Lutherans recognize the sacramentality of ordination to the sacred Ministry? Actually on one occasion in the Lutheran confessional documents,[23] the term 'sacrament' is deemed applicable to ordination, but such language is not common in Lutheran theology. This question is obviously affected by the sixteenth-century dispute about the number of Christian sacraments, a dispute which reflected differences in sacramental theology and in the criteria for defining the term, sacrament. Despite the difference of terminology in reference to the sacramentality of ordination, we have heard our Lutheran partners in the dialogue affirming what to us would be the essentials of Catholic teaching on this subject, namely, that ordination to a sacred Ministry in the church derives from Christ and confers the enduring power to sanctify. We heard the affirmation that 'the Church has the command to appoint Ministers ... God approves the Ministry and is present in it'.[24] 'All three American Lutheran churches understand the Ministry of clergymen to be rooted in the *gospel*'.[25] 'Like the Roman Catholic, the Lutheran too sees ordination as conferring a spiritual authority on the recipient in a once-for-all fashion—namely, the power to sanctify through proclamation ... of the word of God and the administration of the sacraments'.[26]

51. E. Perhaps the most serious obstacle standing in the way of a favourable Catholic evaluation of the Lutheran eucharistic Ministry has been the doctrine of the Council of Trent pertinent to sacred orders. In particular, canon 10 of Session VII (A.D. 1547; DS 1610) denied that all Christians have the power of administering all the sacraments; and canon 7 of Session XXIII (A.D. 1563; DS 1777) said that those who had not been ordained or commissioned by ecclesiastical or canonical power were not legitimate Ministers of the word and the sacraments. It would seem, *prima facie*, that in Trent's judgement Lutheran Ministers, since they have not been ordained by bishops, would not have the power of presiding at the eucharist, and that the Catholic Church could not change its stance on this question since the doctrine of Trent is permanently binding.[27] Yet cautions are in order. The Council of Trent was not concerned primarily with passing judgement on the sacred orders of the Reformed communities but with defending the legitimacy of the Catholic priesthood against Protestant attacks.[28] The Tridentine assessment of Protestant ideas about the Ministry is detected chiefly through the implications of its condemnations of anti-Catholic theories. In the anathemas formulated against 'Those who say . . .' there is no indication of whether Lutherans are meant in distinction from Calvinists, Zwinglians, Anabaptists, etc. Because of these difficulties, it is not easy to determine Trent's attitude toward the Lutheran eucharistic Ministry and the permanent value of that attitude.

52. One approach to the problem is the contention that the Tridentine attitude was not so absolutely negative as has been thought. Some are not sure that the council meant that a Minister 'not ordained by ecclesiastical or canonical power'[29] was really incapable of celebrating the eucharist. They emphasize that all that the council said was that this was not a 'lawful' Ministry.[30] They further point out that the term 'power' is vague in the Tridentine teaching that all Christians do not have the power to celebrate the eucharist, for that word need mean no more than ecclesial authority or authorization.[31]

53. Another approach to the Tridentine position reckons with the likelihood that the council really did mean implicitly to declare

invalid Lutheran orders in the sixteenth century but wonders whether the present situation is not so changed that the Tridentine attitude is now only partially applicable.[32] If Trent rejected the Lutheran Ministry, it did so in the context of what it considered the defective Reformation theology of the Church, the sacraments, and the eucharist. (While we may admit that the Tridentine assessment of these Reformation attitudes was not entirely adequate or correct, we should point out that some of the polemic of the Reformers against the legitimacy of Catholic practices likewise had its share of inadequacies and incorrect assessments—there were weaknesses on both sides.) As is evident from the theological arguments already discussed, we have found in the course of our dialogue with the Lutherans that in the twentieth century there is a much broader agreement on theological questions related to the eucharist than there seems to have been in the sixteenth. Thus the whole context of the discussion of Lutheran Ministry has changed. There is indeed something of permanent value for the Church in Trent's rejection of abuses; but, without settling the question of the past, one might well conclude that the abuses Trent rejected are not present now.

54. The historical and theological reflections made above move us to doubt whether Roman Catholics should continue to question the eucharistic presence of the Lord in the midst of the Lutherans when they meet to celebrate the Lord's supper. And so we make the following statement:

As Roman Catholic theologians, we acknowledge in the spirit of Vatican II that the Lutheran communities with which we have been in dialogue are truly Christian churches, possessing the elements of holiness and truth that mark them as organs of grace and salvation.[33] *Furthermore, in our study we have found serious defects in the arguments customarily used against the validity of the eucharistic Ministry of the Lutheran churches. In fact, we see no persuasive reason to deny the possibility of the Roman Catholic Church recognizing the validity of this Ministry. Accordingly we ask the authorities of the Roman Catholic Church whether the ecumenical urgency flowing from Christ's will for unity*[34] *may not dictate that the Roman Catholic Church recognize the validity of the Lutheran*

Ministry and, correspondingly, the presence of the body and blood of Christ in the eucharistic celebrations of the Lutheran churches.

55. Lest we be misunderstood, we wish to add the following clarifications:

(a) While this statement has implications for the question of Lutheran orders in the past, we have not made that question the focus of our discussions, and we do not think it necessary to solve that problem in order to make the present statement. Nor do we attempt to decide whether recognition by the Roman Catholic Church would be constitutive of validity or merely confirmatory of existing validity.

56. (b) By appealing for *church* action we stress our belief that the problem should be resolved by the respective churches and not on the level of private action by Ministers and priests, for such private action may jeopardize a larger solution.

57. (c) In speaking of the recognition of a Lutheran Ministry not ordained by bishops, we are not in any way challenging the age-old insistence on ordination by a bishop within our own Church or covertly suggesting that it be changed. While we believe that the Church of Jesus Christ is free to adapt the structure of the divinely instituted Ministry in the way she sees fit (so long as the essential meaning and function of apostolic Ministry is retained), we affirm explicitly that the apostolic Ministry is retained in a pre-eminent way in the episcopate, the presbyterate, and the diaconate. We would rejoice if episcopacy in apostolic succession, functioning as the effective sign of church unity, were acceptable to all;[35] but we have envisaged a practical and immediate solution in a *de facto* situation where episcopacy is not yet seen in that light.

58. (d) We do not wish our statement (no. 54) concerning the Lutherans to be thought applicable to others without further and careful consideration, i.e. to other churches, communities, or movements that have the practice of ordination by priests, or where the congregation ordains, or where there is a spontaneous charismatic ministry. Our outlook on the possibilities of accepting

the Lutheran eucharistic Ministry has been greatly determined by our increasing awareness that so much of Lutheran doctrine, practice, and piety is sound from the Catholic viewpoint, particularly in the areas of church, Ministry, and eucharist. Other churches and communities would have to be studied from a similar perspective before one could make a recommendation concerning their Ministries and eucharistic celebrations.

59. (e) We caution that we have not discussed the implications that a recognition of valid Ministry would have for intercommunion or eucharistic sharing. Obviously recognition of valid Ministry and sharing the eucharistic table are intimately related, but we are not in a position to affirm that the one must or should lead to the other. At the same time, we note that the *Ecumenical Directory*, promulgated by the Vatican Secretariat for Christian Unity, states that Catholics in circumstances involving sufficient reason or urgent cause may receive the sacraments of the holy eucharist, penance, and the anointing of the sick from one who has been 'validly ordained'.[36]

PARTICIPANTS

ROMAN CATHOLIC

The Most Revd T. Austin Murphy, Auxiliary Bishop of Baltimore, Maryland

Dr Thomas E. Ambrogi, Professor of Religious Studies, University of the Pacific, Stockton, California*

The Revd Mgr Joseph W. Baker, Vice-Chairman of the Ecumenical Commission of the Archdiocese of St Louis, Missouri

The Most Revd William W. Baum, Bishop of Springfield-Cape Girardeau, Missouri

The Revd Fr Raymond E. Brown, ss, Professor of Sacred Scripture, St Mary's Seminary, Baltimore, Maryland

The Revd Fr Walter J. Burghardt, sj, Professor of Patristics, Woodstock College, New York

The Revd Fr Godfrey Dickmann, osb, Professor of Patristics, St John's Abbey, Collegeville, Minnesota

The Revd Fr Maurice C. Duchaine, ss, Professor of Dogmatic Theology, St Mary's Seminary, Baltimore, Maryland

The Revd Fr John F. Hotchkin, Associate Director, Bishops' Committee for Ecumenical and Interreligious Affairs, Washington, D.C.

Professor James F. McCue, School of Religion, University of Iowa, Iowa City, Iowa

The Revd Fr Kilian McDonnell, osb, Executive Director, Institute for Ecumenical and Cultural Research, Collegeville, Minnesota

Dr Harry J. McSorley, Professor of Ecumenical Theology, St Paul's College, Washington, DC.

The Revd Fr Anthony T. Padovano, Professor of Dogmatic Theology, Immaculate Conception Seminary, Darlington, New Jersey

The Revd Fr Jerome D. Quinn, Professor of Old and New Testament, The St Paul Seminary, St Paul, Minnesota

The Revd Fr George H. Tavard, AA, Visiting Professor, Methodist Theological School, Delaware, Ohio

* Participated in first two sessions only

LUTHERAN

Dr Paul C. Empie, General Secretary, USA National Committee of the Lutheran World Federation, New York, New York

Dr Kent S. Knutson, President, Wartburg Theological Seminary, Dubuque, Iowa

Dr Fred Kramer, Professor of Systematic Theology, Concordia Theological Seminary, Springfield, Illinois

Dr George A. Lindbeck, Professor of Historical Theology, Yale University Divinity School, New Haven, Connecticut

Dr Paul D. Opsahl, Associate Executive Secretary, Division of Theological Studies, Lutheran Council in the USA, New York

Dr Arthur Carl Piepkorn, Graduate Professor of Systematic Theology, Concordia Seminary, St Louis, Missouri

Dr Warren A. Quanbeck, Professor of Systematic Theology, Luther Theological Seminary, St Paul, Minnesota

Dr John Reumann, Professor of New Testament, The Lutheran Seminary, Philadelphia, Pennsylvania

Dr Joseph Sittler, Professor of Theology, University of Chicago Divinity School, Chicago, Illinois

NOTES

PART ONE

1. For the distinction between *Ministry* and *ministry*, see para. 9 below.
2. *The Status of the Nicene Creed as Dogma of the Church*, USA National Committee of the Lutheran World Federation and the Bishops' Commission for Ecumenical Affairs, 1965.
3. *Lutherans and Catholics in Dialogue II: One Baptism for the Remission of Sins;* ed. Paul C. Empie and William W. Baum. USA National Committee of the Lutheran World Federation and the Bishops' Commission for Ecumenical Affairs, 1966.
4. *Lutherans and Catholics in Dialogue III: The Eucharist as Sacrifice.* USA National Committee of the Lutheran World Federation and the Bishops' Committee for Ecumenical and Interreligious Affairs, 1967. Also in *Modern Eucharistic Agreement* (SPCK 1973), p. 33.
5. *Faith and Order Findings,* Montreal, 1963 (Minneapolis, 1963).
6. Development of the Ministry of the Christian Church is difficult to trace and much controverted. Cf. Jerome D. Quinn, 'Ministry in the New Testament', in *Lutherans and Catholics in Dialogue IV* (hereafter called *LCD IV*), pp. 69–100. The passages cited in the text above list the following varieties of ministering:

1 Corinthians 12: apostles, prophets, teachers, miracle-workers, healers, administrators, those who speak in tongues;
Romans 12: prophecy, serving (*diakonia*), teaching, exhorting, liberality in giving, zeal in aid, acts of mercy;
Ephesians 4: apostles, prophets, evangelists, pastors, teachers.

Everyone would agree that some of these categories belong in the special Ministry of the Church (e.g. apostles, prophets, teachers), and that others reflect the ministry of the people of God (acts of mercy, aid, and helping), and that some are hard to categorize (healing, teaching). Of particular interest, in any sketch of the development, would be the Ministry of 'the Twelve', the Ministry of the apostles in a broader sense, the Ministry of the presbyter-bishop, the Ministry of those who baptized, and the Ministry of those who presided at the eucharist. Information, however, is incomplete. Neither the Twelve nor the apostles in the Pauline writings seem to have limited their Ministry to a local church as the later presbyter-bishop normally did, nor do we have much evidence of their administering sacraments. In fact, we are told very little in the New Testament about those who did preside at the eucharist. Thus the Ministry in the later Church involving evangelism, preaching, sacraments, pastoral care, and administration in a community, combines functions that were not always united in the early Church.

7. Cf. the paper given at the Catholic-Lutheran conversations in Nemi, Italy, May 1969, by George A. Lindbeck, 'The Lutheran Doctrine of the Ministry: Catholic and Reformed', in *Theological Studies* 30 (1969), pp. 588–612; also the Common Statement of the Nemi meeting.

8. Warren A. Quanbeck, 'A Contemporary View of Apostolic Succession', in *LCD IV*, pp. 185–7.

9. James F. McCue, 'Apostles and Apostolic Succession in the Patristic Era', pp. 173–7 and Walter J. Burghardt, 'Apostolic Succession: Notes on the Early Patristic Era', both in *LCD IV*.

10. The variety of ways in which the term 'apostolic' is applied is not startling when we note that the New Testament authors employ the term 'apostle' to designate persons with a variety of roles in the earliest Christian generations (cf. R. Schnackenburg, 'L'apostolicité: état de la recherche', in *Istina* 14 (1969), 5–32, a paper originally prepared for the Vatican–World Council of Churches discussions on 'Apostolicity and Catholicity'.

The Second Vatican Council Decree on Ecumenism twice adverts to the fact that variety is itself an element in apostolicity. 'While preserving unity in essentials, let all members of the Church, according to the office entrusted to each, preserve a proper freedom in the various forms of spiritual life and discipline, in the variety of liturgical rites, and even in the theological elaboration of revealed truth. In all things let charity be exercised. If the faithful are true to this course of action, they will be giving ever richer expression to the authentic catholicity of the Church, and, at the same time, to her apostolicity' (4).

This principle finds its first and obvious application in relation to the churches of the East and the Council Fathers emphatically reaffirmed it when they said, '. . . this Sacred Synod declares that this entire heritage of (Eastern) spirituality and liturgy, of discipline and theology, in their various traditions, belongs to the full Catholic and apostolic character of the Church' (17).

Our Lutheran-Catholic dialogue has been conscious of and attempted to implement this principle as we sorted out our answers to the question, 'How is the Ministry apostolic?'

11. Burghardt, op. cit.

12. Cf. the Lutheran replies to Catholic questions, Baltimore sessions, given by George A. Lindbeck and Warren A. Quanbeck, pp. 53–60.

13. Denzinger-Schönmetzer, *Enchiridion Symbolorum*, 33rd edn (hereafter cited as DS) (Freiburg 1965), 1609; cf. 1313.

14. George A. Lindbeck, 'The Lutheran Doctrine of the Ministry: Catholic and Reformed', cited above, note 7; article, *Ordo*, by Piet Fransen, in *Lexikon für Theologie und Kirche*, vol. 7 (Freiburg 1962), columns 1215, 1216; article 'Orders and Ordination', by Piet Fransen, in *Sacramentum Mundi*, vol. 4 (NY 1969), pp. 305–27.

15. The *Dogmatic Constitution on the Church* (*Lumen Gentium*) of Vatican II states, 'This sacred Synod teaches that by episcopal consecration is conferred the fulness of the sacrament of orders (*plenitudinem conferri sacramenti Ordinis*), that fulness which in the Church's liturgical practice and in the language of the holy Fathers of the Church is undoubtedly called the high priesthood, the apex of the sacred ministry' (21). The Council Fathers were first asked whether they wished to say that episcopal consecration constituted the *summum gradum sacramenti Ordinis*. After agreeing upon this, the precise terminology for expressing it was debated. As the *Relatio* of 1964 puts it, '*Potius autem quam supremus gradus sacramenti Ordinis, Episcopatus dicendus est eius plentitudo seu totalitas, omnes partes includens . . .; plenitudo sacerdotii cui presbyteri deinde participant . . .; plenitudo sacramenti Ordinis, vel ipsum sacramentum Ordinis*'. (Rather than the highest degree of the sacrament of orders, the episcopate should be called its fulness or totality, embracing all its parts . . .; the fulness of priesthood in which priests then participate . . .; the fulness of the sacrament of orders, or the sacrament of orders itself.)

16. DS 1145–1146, 1290. Cf. Fransen, 'Orders and Ordination', in *Sacramentum Mundi*, vol. 4, esp. p. 316; Kilian McDonnell, 'Ways

of Validating Ministry', *Journal of Ecumenical Studies* 7 (1970), pp. 209–65; A. C. Piepkorn, 'The Sacred Ministry and Holy Ordination in the Symbolical Books of the Lutheran Church', in *LCD IV*, pp. 116–17.

17. In Lutheran churches, for pastoral and administrative reasons, one pastor is designated 'pastor of pastors', president of district or synod, or bishop. See Piepkorn, op. cit. See also the 'Reflections of the Lutheran Participants' below.

18. *Apology of the Augsburg Confession*, Article 14. The critical edition of the Lutheran confessions is *Die Bekenntnisschriften der evangelischlutherischen Kirche* (6th edn, Göttingen 1967). The standard English edition is *The Book of Concord: The Confessions of the Evangelical Lutheran Church;* ed. by Theodore G. Tappert (Philadelphia, 1959). Cf. below the Lutheran answer to the Catholic question at the Baltimore sessions, 'How do Lutherans evaluate, theologically and practically, episcopally structured churches?' pp. 53–6. Cf. also no. 28 of the Lutheran 'Reflections' below.

19. Other aspects of matters treated need further discussion and many other topics are not touched in these common observations. Among the latter might be mentioned the apostolic Ministry and succession of the bishop of Rome and its relationship to the apostleship of Peter and Paul; infallibility, especially as applied to papal infallibility; the distinction between matters that are of divine law and those which are of human law (*jure divino et humano*); the question of a purely charismatic ministry; questions of eucharistic sharing; the specific relations of a presbyterally ordained Ministry to an episcopally oriented Ministry; and finally, the practical problems of mutual recognition of Ministries, including psychological, canonical, and administrative factors.

NOTES

PART TWO

1. *Augsburg Confession*, Epilogue to Article 21, 1–5; Preface to Article 22, 1; Postscript to Article 28. See also *Apology of the Augsburg Confession*, 2, 32; 10, 2–3.

2. 'Sacraments' in this connection include at least baptism, absolution conceived of either as implied in baptism or as an independent sacrament and the sacrament of the altar.

3. *Augsburg Confession*, 5, 1–3; 7, 1–4; 14; **28, 5–9,** 21–2; *Apology*, 28, 13.

4. *Apology*, 4, 211.

5. *Large Catechism*, Baptism, 50.

6. *Decree on Ecumenism*, 20.

7. *Augsburg Confession*, 20, 40, recalls that 'the church sings: "*Sine tuo numine / Nihil est in homine, / Nihil est innoxium*" ' (Without [the action of] your godhead, there is nothing in a human being, there is nothing that is not destructive), from the *Veni, Sancte Spiritus*.
8. *Apology*, 14, 1. 5.
9. In the technical sense of an unbroken personal succession of members of the episcopal order theoretically going back to the apostles, with each bishop consecrated to the episcopal order by one or more persons already in the order.
10. The focus of Lutheran concern in the sixteenth century (Smalcald Articles, Part Two, 4, 4. 10–12) was the concluding definition of *Unam Sanctam: Porro subesse Romano Pontifici omni humanae creaturae declaramus, dicimus, diffinimus omnino esse de necessitate salutis* (Further, we declare, state [and] define that for every human being it is absolutely necessary for salvation to be under the bishop of Rome) (DS 875). We have not discussed the papacy with our Roman Catholic partners-in-dialogue, but we look forward to an examination of this issue at an early date. In the meantime, however, it may be observed that, however widely the cited thesis of Boniface VIII may have been held during the three centuries following its promulgation in 1302, it runs counter to twentieth-century Roman Catholic thought (see, for instance, the letter of the Holy Office to the Cardinal Archbishop of Boston dated 8 August 1949, of which DS 3866–73 reproduces the essential portions). Similarly, the recognition sanctioned by Vatican II that the 'churches and ecclesial communities' that are not in communion with the Roman see are not without 'significance and importance in the mystery of salvation', that the Holy Spirit uses these churches and ecclesial communities 'as means of salvation', and that Roman Catholics are to regard 'all those justified by faith through baptism [as] incorporated into Christ' and as 'brothers in the Lord' may be read as a kind of modern modification of the passage in *Unam Sanctam* that Lutherans have found so disconcerting (*Decree on Ecumenism*, 3). We also note that in the Dogmatic Constitution on the Church, 15, 'communion with the successor of Peter' is not a necessary prerequisite in the case of baptized persons for being 'honoured with the name of Christian', for being 'united with Christ', and for receiving 'other sacraments'. Again, the entire section on 'The Separated Churches and Ecclesial Communities in the West' in the Decree on Ecumenism (19–23) nowhere mentions the papacy as such. At most it speaks of 'the churches and ecclesial communities which were separated from the Apostolic See of Rome' and 'the ecclesial communities separated from us'. Also relevant to this issue is the fact that the Roman Catholic Church recognizes as authentic churches the Eastern Orthodox bodies that have consistently refused to acknowledge a divine-right universal jurisdiction of the pope (Decreee on Ecumenism, 14–18).

11. Smalcald Articles, Part Two, 4, 1, '*Dass der Papst nicht sei* jure divino *oder aus Gottes Wort das Haupt der ganzen Christenheit (denn das gehoret einem allein zu, der heisst Jesus Christus), sondern allein Bischof oder Pfarrher der Kirchen zu Rom....*'. (The pope is not the head of all Christendom by divine right or according to God's Word, for this position belongs only to one, namely, to Jesus Christ. The pope is only the bishop and pastor of the churches in Rome....)

12. Ibid., 7–8. We have as yet not had the opportunity to discuss with our Roman Catholic counterparts the full significance of the terms *jure divino* and *jure humano*.

13. For example, in the *Decree on the Ministry and Life of Priests*, 4.

14. In this dialogue (but cf. *Lutherans and Catholics in Dialogue III: The Eucharist as Sacrifice*, p. 191, *Modern Eucharistic Agreement*, hereafter called *MEA*, p. 39) we have not discussed the matter of 'private masses', which Lutherans have regarded as an abuse (cf. Smalcald Articles, Part Two, 2, 8). We rejoice that current Roman Catholic theology emphasizes the communal aspects of the eucharist.

15. Instruction on Eucharistic Worship (25 May 1967), p. 49, cited in *Lutherans and Catholics in Dialogue III: The Eucharist as Sacrifice*, p. 194; *MEA*, p. 41.

16. Ibid., pp. 188–98 (the quotation is from p. 196). This sentence from the conclusion is particularly apposite (p. 198): 'Despite all remaining differences in the ways we speak and think of the eucharistic sacrifice and our Lord's presence in his supper, we are no longer able to regard ourselves as divided in the one holy catholic and apostolic faith on these two points.'

17. For example, the examination of what the anathemas of Trent and of Vatican I (DS 3055, 3058, 3064, and 3075) and the exceedingly severe judgements on dissenters from the definitions of 1854 (DS 2804) and 1950 (DS 3904) really imply. These are occasions of concern to Lutherans, since they apparently exclude large numbers of sincere believers from the Church. Indeed, they exclude so many believers that they seem to some Lutherans to call into question the churchly character of the community that pronounces them. We anticipate a thorough discussion of this problem with our Roman Catholic colleagues.

18. See the *Decree on the Bishops' Pastoral Office in the Church*, 12, and the *Dogmatic Constitution on the Church*, 21.

NOTES
PART THREE

1. See the Lutheran answers given to Catholic questions at the Baltimore sessions, pp. 53–61. Cf. no. 21 above.

2. We do not wish to discuss here or elsewhere in this document the preservation of pre-Reformation episcopal structure in the Lutheran Church of Sweden, Finland, and some missionary churches. See the Lutheran answer at the Baltimore sessions, question 1, section 3, p. 55. In general, what we say in this document of the Lutherans or the Lutheran communities refers to those Lutheran communities with whose representatives we have been in dialogue. Cf. no. 28 above.

3. Cf. R. Schnackenburg, 'L'apostolicité', as cited above, Chapter 1, note 10.

4. The Didache is a work of uncertain date, perhaps even first century. James F. McCue, 'Apostles and Apostolic Succession in the Patristic Era', in *LCD IV*, pp. 163–4, interprets Tertullian, *de exh. cast.* 7 (early third century) to mean that in cases of necessity the eucharist might be celebrated by an unordained layman.

5. A. C. Piepkorn, 'A Lutheran View of the Validity of Lutheran Orders', in *LCD IV*, pp. 217–19.

6. Session XXIII, canon 7; DS 1777. See Piepkorn, op. cit., p. 220.

7. Piepkorn, op. cit., pp. 220–6; Corrado Baisi, *Il ministro straordinario degli ordini sacramentali* (Rome 1935); Yves Congar, 'Faits, problèmés, et réflexions à propos du pouvoir d'ordre et des rapports entre le presbytérat et l'épiscopat', in *Sacramentum Mundi*, NY, vol. 4 (1969), p. 316; the full texts of the bulls may be found in H. Lennerz, *de Sacramento Ordinis, editio secunda* (Rome, 1953).

8. *Constitution on the Church (Lumen Gentium)*, 15; *Decree on Ecumenism*, 3

9. Kilian McDonnell, 'The Concept of "Church" in the Documents of Vatican II as Applied to Protestant Denominations', in *LCD IV*, pp. 307–24.

10. *Constitution on the Church*, 15. Speaking of Christian churches that do not preserve the unity of communion with the successor of Peter, Vatican II states, 'Many of them . . . celebrate the Holy Eucharist'.

11. Cf. note 2, above.

12. Walter J. Burghardt, 'Apostolic Succession: Notes on the Early Patristic Era', in *LCD IV*, pp. 713–17.

13. Ibid.; see also McCue, op. cit., pp. 156–7.

14. In the joint Lutheran-Roman Catholic document, *The Status of the Nicene Creed as Dogma of the Church* (1965), p. 32, both sides confess that 'the Nicene Faith possesses a unique status in the hierarchy of dogmas', and it is that creed which proclaims the church as one, holy, catholic, and *apostolic*.

15. *Lutherans and Catholics in Dialogue III: The Eucharist as Sacrifice*, pp. 192, 188; *MEA*, pp. 30, 40, 37.

16. Cf. Piepkorn, 'The Sacred Ministry and Holy Ordination in the Symbolical Books of the Lutheran Church', p. 102, section 4.

17. Cf. ibid., p. 116, section 25.
18. Ibid., p. 105, section 8; cf. pp. 107–8, section 12.
19. John Reumann, 'Ordained Minister and Layman in Lutheranism', sections 16–18, 28–30, 44, in *LCD IV*, pp. 235, 239–40, 247–8.
20. *Constitution on the Church*, 10: *Essentia enim et non gradu tantum inter se differunt.* (Though they differ from one another in essence and not only in degree); for discussions of these, see *Commentary on the Documents of Vatican II;* ed. Herbert Vorgrimler (NY 1967), pp. 156–9, and John F. Hotchkin, 'The Christian Priesthood: Episcopate, Presbyterate and People in the Light of Vatican II', pp. 202–6.
21. *Augsburg Confession*, 14: *De ordine ecclesiastico docent, quod nemo debeat in ecclesia publice docere aut sacramenta administrare nisi rite vocatus'.* (Our churches teach that nobody in the Church should publicly preach or administer the sacraments unless he is regularly called); *Apology*, 14, 1: *Dicimus nemini nisi rite vocato concedendam esse administrationem sacramentorum et verbi in ecclesia.* (We say that no one should be allowed to administer the word and the sacraments in the church unless he is duly called); see Piepkorn, op. cit., pp. 113–16, section 23, for a discussion of *rite vocatus*.
22. The concept of royal priesthood is found in Exodus 19. 6: I Peter 2. 9; Revelation 5. 9–10. A recent Lutheran work, John H. Elliott, *The Elect and the Holy*, Supplements to *Novum Testamentum* 12 (Leiden 1966), has examined I Peter 2. 9 carefully and finds no evidence that the author of that biblical book related this priesthood to the eucharistic Ministry. The *Constitution on the Church*, 10, says, 'The faithful join in the offering of the eucharist by virtue of their royal priesthood'.
23. *Apology*, 13, 9–13; see Reumann, op. cit., sections 25–6, p. 238; Piepkorn, op. cit., p. 112, section 21.
24. Cf. Reumann, section 26, p. 238.
25. Cf. ibid., section 73, p. 265.
26. Piepkorn, 'A Lutheran View of the Validity of Lutheran Orders', in *LCD IV*, p. 215. It should be noted that one who resigns from the Lutheran ministry and then seeks readmission to the exercise of the Ministry is not reordained. Cf. Piepkorn, 'The Sacred Ministry', p. 117, section 26.
27. For a variety of possible Catholic reactions to the Tridentine and Counter-Reformation positions, see George H. Tavard, 'Roman Catholic Theology and Recognition of Ministry', in *LCD IV*, pp. 301–5.
28. It argues on behalf of a visible and sacramental priesthood that has a perpetual character, on behalf of an episcopate and the pope's right to appoint bishops, and on behalf of the validity of ordination by a bishop.

29. DS 1777. Note the wording; it is significant that Trent ignored a proposal which stated that only those ordained *by bishops* are legitimate Ministers of the eucharist.

30. Harry J. McSorley, 'Trent and the Question: Can Protestant ministers Consecrate the Eucharist?' in *LCD IV*, especially pp. 291–3. On p. 293, he contends, 'It seems to us that Trent is asserting the canonical or juridical illegitimacy (illiceity) of Lutheran ordinations—not their invalidity in a widely held modern sense'.

31. Ibid., pp. 283–5, 294–5. It should be noted that there was disagreement among the Catholic participants in regard to this position.

32. Particularly involved here is the question of hermeneutics, and the nature of the Church's grasp of truth in any era.

33. See the *Constitution on the Church*, 8 and 15 (with the *relatio specialis* to 15), and the *Decree on Ecumenism*, 19–23.

34. Our intention here echoes the assurance of Cardinal Willebrands, President of the Vatican Secretariat for Christian Unity, when, in speaking of the divisions which still remain, he declares '. . . our firm resolve to do everything possible to overcome them' ('The Position of the Catholic Church concerning a Common Eucharist between Christians of Different Confessions', 7 January 1970, see *One in Christ* 6 (1970), p. 201, no. 10).

35. See the Lutheran answer to a Catholic question, given at the Baltimore sessions, pp. 56–60.

36. *Directory for the Application of the Decisions of the Second Ecumenical Council of the Vatican Concerning Ecumenical Matters*. (Secretariat for Promoting Christian Unity (Washington, DC, United States Catholic Conference, 1967), p. 55.)

Group of Les Dombes

TOWARDS A RECONCILIATION OF MINISTRIES

Points of Agreement between Roman Catholics and Protestants

TRANSLATED BY
Pamela Gaughan

First published 1973
in French with the title
Pour une réconciliation des ministères
by Les Presses de Taizé
71460 Taizé-Communauté, France

© Groupe des Dombes 1973

© Translation, SPCK 1975

PREAMBLE

The text that the Group of Les Dombes is publishing this year (1973) is designed to meet the pastoral need already discussed in the doctrinal agreement on the eucharist published last year.[1] 'For some years past, the Group meeting at Les Dombes has been scrutinizing the significance of mutual eucharistic hospitality and joint celebration and the conditions on which they depend.'

Whereas the doctrinal agreement on the eucharist concentrated on one essential condition of mutual eucharistic hospitality, namely, a substantial agreement on what the eucharist is, the text we are presenting here invites the churches to recognize each other's ministries and so give a theological and ecclesial basis to joint celebrations of the eucharist. The first part of the text is thus devoted to the theological foundations, that is to say, to establishing points of agreement in regard to the ministry. The ecclesial foundation—making proposals of an exploratory nature with a view to a reconciliation of ministries—is the subject of the second part.

First, let us specify the limits of the doctrinal agreement: the text 'demonstrates a fundamental agreement between us regarding the nature and significance of the pastoral ministry in the mystery of the Church'. It does not broach questions of the form and organization of the ministry, but the diversity of forms does not seem to us necessarily an obstacle in the way of a reconciliation. Surely the essential thing is our common understanding of the relationship of ministers to Jesus Christ and to the Church, of the significance of their ordination and of their role in the life of Christian communities.

It was in 1957 that the Group embarked on a systematic study of this question which caused such a serious cleavage between the Catholic Church and the churches of the Reformation that it produced in the West two distinct types of minister: the priest and the pastor. During the fifteen succeeding years, the Group has taken a large part in the multiple researches undertaken in this field which, since Vatican II, has become one of the chief concerns in the life of the churches. Let us look back over the principal stages in the Group's thinking on the subject.

The starting-point was the fact that 'Jesus Christ is the one mediator between God and man'; 'the ministry of the Church consists in bringing all men back to this unique mediation which "manifests itself in the signs of the Word and the Sacraments".' All thinking about the ministry is bound up basically with the Church's mission 'in the service of man'.

This requires us to define the relationship between Christ and the Church. Reflecting in 1958 on the doctrine of the Body of Christ, we identified a twofold relationship: 'Jesus Christ is the head of this body in such a way that his organic unity with his Church does not affect his supremacy over it'. The ministries are destined to partake of this twofold relationship and hence, in 1959, we placed the authority of the minister 'within the framework of fraternal relations among the baptized'. Christ, supreme Pastor of his Church, exercises his authority through ministers empowered by him', which means that the authority of the minister is part of the Church's very being but the ministry derives its authority from the fact of being 'the service of Christ in the power of the Spirit'. This diaconal character of the ministry is forcefully stressed.

We were ready now to look at the two most delicate questions: the apostolic succession (1960) and the sacerdotal character of the ministry (1961 and 1962). While these sessions may not have enabled us to overcome our differences, they defined them and produced affirmations which were significant for the rest of our work. Let us mention in particular the distinction between the non-transmissible features of the apostolate: the testimony of eye-witnesses, the foundation on which the Lord built his Church; and the transmissible features: the command to proclaim the gospel and to establish the Church. Let us underline also our affirmation that 'the Body of Christ, the High Priest, manifests itself and fulfils itself as a sacerdotal body', when Christ, giving himself to the Church in the eucharist, 'identifies it with his own movement towards the Father' and thus makes it 'participate in his praise of the Father and in his powerful intercession for the salvation of the world'.

But the meeting in 1963 to assess our progress made us realize that this Christological thinking had to be counterbalanced by Pneumatological thinking. This latter, conducted with the eminently enlightening participation of Paul Evdokimov in the years 1965–66–67, allowed us once more to take up our research on the subject of the ministries. We began in 1967 with the question of the presidency of the eucharist, which we considered in 1968 in the specific light of the study of the Irenaean doctrine of the apostolic succession and its relationship to the eucharist; lastly, our research comprised reflections on ordination, the relationship between ministry and charism and between ministry and prophecy and looked ahead to a possible reconciliation of the different ministries. It was at the 1972 meeting that all these separate elements were embodied in the text we are presenting here.

While this text does not deal with the difficulties arising from the organization of the different ministries, it should be pointed out that the 1970 'theses' give some idea of the changes we feel are necessary, on the Catholic as well as on the Protestant side. Other points that should be stressed are our statements regarding the 'co-responsibility of all Christians' expressing itself in diverse and complementary ministries (paragraphs 18, 19), on the forms of ordained ministry which 'may vary according to the needs of the Church and the mission it entrusts to its ministers' and the rejection of the concept of a 'clerical caste' (paragraph 36).

Part Two of our text no doubt suffers from the speed with which it was drawn up, at the end of a particularly busy session. For this reason, the members of the Group, rather than signing it, preferred to record that they had contributed to its drafting. While it is in the nature of a proposition susceptible of amendment and improvement, it is nevertheless inseparable from the doctrinal agreement, since it bears witness to the Group's determination to be at the service of God's people in this call for action to transform situations which for too long have remained fixed and unchanging in separation. What use would it be to progress in mutual understanding of the salvation brought by Christ, of the mission he has entrusted to his Church, of the manner in which he wishes his Church to be built and equipped for its mission, if it did not enable us the better to carry out that mission together?

INTRODUCTION

1. In pouring out his liberating love, God chose a people called to bear witness, through its history, to a promise given to all men.

This servant-people is called to be at all times and in all places a sign of hope along the path trodden by man.

This mission makes God's people one with all mankind and we are still the beneficiaries today of that *prophetic call*.

2. Into the midst of this people God sends his Son, to be the servant of his fellow-men and to reveal to man the reality of salvation.

Jesus Christ is thus the one Lord and Saviour who, by giving his life for men, calls them, through his service, to discover the meaning of their existence and the fulness of a new humanity.

3. The power of his resurrection is manifested from generation to generation by the action of the Holy Spirit, who inspires the Church, calls it together in thanksgiving, and sends it forth on the mission entrusted to it.

This mission commits the whole of God's people to service that demands fidelity, perseverance, and effectiveness.

4. This is why, listening with renewed attention to the apostolic message and its promise for mankind, we are endeavouring today to discern the calls of the Holy Spirit.

In ecumenical research, in particular where the ministry of the Church and ministries within the Church are concerned, the fundamental criterion must be apostolicity, seen as both source and mission.

This research not only concerns and sheds light on the internal life of the Church, but it prepares and qualifies the Church for the fulfilment of Christ's mission.

Part One
POINTS OF AGREEMENT REGARDING THE MINISTRY

I
CHRIST, LORD AND SERVANT, SOLE MINISTER OF HIS CHURCH

5. It is impossible to speak of the ministry of the Church and in the Church without first speaking of the ministry of Jesus Christ himself. The ministry which he exercised by his life and death, the risen Christ is still carrying on in and for his Church today, so that it may serve him among the men of our time.

6. The ministry of Christ is the norm of all doctrine and all practice of the Christian ministry—a ministry which, in all its variety of institutional forms, demands a constantly renewed fidelity to Christ's example. 'Yet here I am among you as one who serves', says Jesus (Luke 22. 27); 'I have given you an example so that you may copy what I have done to you' (John 13. 15); and again: 'If a man serves me, he must follow me; wherever I am my servant will be there too' (John 12. 26).[2]

7. Jesus Christ himself, mysteriously present to his Church, challenges it constantly through his word and his Spirit to examine itself and remain faithful to its vocation and mission. To 'follow' Christ and become like him is also an integral part of the apostolic succession.

II

THE CHURCH OF CHRIST: CHURCH OF THE APOSTLES

8. The Church, body of Christ, is apostolic in its very essence, because Christ, sent by the Father, sends the Church in turn into the world in the power of the Spirit.

9. The whole Church, summoned by Christ, is sent to summon all men to the eschatological assembly of salvation. This means that the whole Church has a mission and therefore a ministry. So that the Church may fulfil this mission, Christ has given it, in the person of the apostles, the ministerial sign that it is he who is calling. This is why the apostolic character of the Church comprises two inseparable aspects:

10. The apostolicity of the Church is founded on Christ's fidelity to his promise to be always with his people and on the presence and action of the Holy Spirit, who is building it up day by day. There is, therefore, an apostolic succession of the whole Church.

11. But within that apostolic succession Christ, in order to manifest his initiative of grace, to guarantee the transcendence of the apostolic message, and to ensure the fulfilment of the Church's mission, sent his apostles as his envoys, thanks to the gift of the Holy Spirit. In the wake of the apostles, the apostolic ministry is still being carried on in the Church on the foundation which they constituted and it must remain entirely faithful to the message they have transmitted. This ministry—a gift of God for the service of the whole Church—forms part of the Church's structure. There is, therefore, an apostolic succession in the ministry instituted by our Lord.

12. The fulness of the apostolic succession of the whole Church implies continuity in the essential features of the Church of the apostles: witness to the faith, fraternal communion, sacramental life, service of mankind, dialogue with the world, and the sharing of the gifts which God has given to each member.

13. The fulness of the apostolic succession in the ministry implies continuity in the transmission of the ministerial function, fidelity in preaching to the teaching of the apostles, and a life in keeping with the gospel and the demands of mission. These three features are usually inseparable.

This succession, in fact, as a ministerial sign, bears witness to the apostolic character of the Church and prepares the community for the coming and the action of our Lord himself.

III
THE MINISTRY OF THE WHOLE CHURCH AND THE DIVERSITY OF MINISTRIES WITHIN THE CHURCH

14. The common mission of the Church, attested by the Gospels, is entrusted to each Christian by baptism with water and the Holy Spirit and by his participation in the eucharist.

15. Each member of the body of Christ is called and empowered to live his faith and bear witness to it among his fellows by serving love and justice and by radiating hope. Thus the Christian community in each place bears witness to the reconciliation whereby it lives and calls on all men to be reconciled with God and with one another.

16. At all times and in all places, the Church, God's people, is, despite its unworthiness, 'a chosen race, a royal priesthood, a consecrated nation, a people set apart to sing the praises of God', who called men 'into his wonderful light' (1 Peter 2. 9).

17. Preaching the gospel, the Church's service to the world, and the building up of the community all require very different activities, permanent or temporary, spontaneous or institutionalized.

18. Thus, the Holy Spirit calls men and women from among God's people to take on different and complementary ministries which all bear witness to Christ's fidelity to his promises and to the richness of his gifts.

19. From this it can be seen that witness and service in the cause of Christ are not the monopoly of a few but the co-responsibility of all Christians.

IV
PASTORAL MINISTRY AND COMMUNITY:
THEIR DEPENDENCE ON CHRIST

20. Whatever the diversity of charisms and functions in a Christian community, the mark of the pastoral ministry[3] is to ensure and signify the Church's dependence on Christ, a source of its mission and foundation of its unity.

21. Though he is himself a member of the Christian community, a minister is at the same time to be recognized as an envoy whom that community receives from Christ. The minister's functions bring out the priority in the life of the Church of divine initiative and authority, the continuity of the mission in the world, the bond of communion established by the Spirit in the different communities in the unity of the Church.

This implies the minister's membership, with ministers of other times and other places, of the same 'college',[4] deriving from the apostles.

22. This relationship of dependence on the one Lord and Saviour is expressed and lived out in the dependence of the community and the minister on one another. Their mutual dependence shows that the Church is not in a position of mastery over the word and the sacraments, nor is it the source of its own faith, hope, and unity and that the minister, for his part, does not exist by or for himself, nor can he dispose as he wishes of the Christian community.

Thus, the Christian life and the ministry are received from Another—Christ living in his Church. They are animated by his Spirit and subject to his judgement.

23. The pastoral ministry, which will endure until Christ's Parousia, is also a prophetic ministry: its apostolic origin and its

foundation on the authority of our Lord, far from justifying a possessive, inward-looking attitude, oblige it to turn towards the future, which it heralds.

24. The relationships which establish themselves between the ministry and the community in the unity of the Church reflect those between the persons of the Trinity in the divine Unity: ministry and community find their source of authority in the person of the Father, of their service in the person of the Son and of their freedom and communion in the person of the Holy Spirit.

V
EXERCISE OF THE PASTORAL MINISTRY

25. The essential functions of the pastoral ministry, which inherits the transmissible features of the apostolic function, are indissolubly bound up with one another: proclamation of the Word, celebration of the sacraments, and calling together of the community.

26. By the ministry of the Word, Christ feeds the Church with the gospel whereby it lives and constantly reveals its riches so that they may be passed on to all men.

This ministry does not stop short at repeating what has already been said long ago; it interprets it and makes it real, guided in this by the Holy Spirit in the communion of the whole Church. It also endeavours to identify the points where the message of Jesus Christ and the problems, situations, and culture of the modern world meet one another or, on the contrary, set up tensions.

27. By the ministry of the sacraments, Christ passes on the gift of his person and of his life. In celebrating the sacraments, the minister signifies that it is Christ himself who presides and gives them the efficacy he has promised. He demonstrates too that the word of the gospel is at work in the sacrament, fulfilling what it has announced. By this means the communion of the Church with the Holy Spirit, its life as the body of Christ, and its fidelity to God are established and renewed.

28. Through the ministry of calling together the community, Christ is constantly restoring and building up his people's unity in their progress towards the Kingdom. This ministry is exercised with respect for the freedom of the Holy Spirit and recognition of the real common responsibility of all Christians.

29. The pastoral ministry, in its three functions, derives its authority from the fact that it is the service of Christ who, as Lord and Head of his body, sets it up in the power of the Spirit.

30. In these three functions of the ministry, the relationship of authority is still present in brotherly love and the shared responsibility of Christian people sent forth into the world by Christ. Thus the faithful and their ministers are bound one to another in different relationships of interdependence and reciprocity.

By dialogue and by prayer, those who celebrate in different contexts the same sacrament are one in opening their hearts to the Holy Spirit.

The questions raised by the life of Christian people, their witness, and their understanding of the message of the gospel, educate the ministers of the word, and clarify for them the meaning of the faith, whose servants they are.

31. Within the priesthood of the baptized, Christ gives his Church its structure, thanks to the pastoral ministry through which he leads his disciples to spiritual sacrifice, witness, and service along many roads which, as it were, meet and cross in the eucharist. It is in this sense that the ministry is said to be sacerdotal.

32. God expresses his fidelity to his Church by the support he gives to the ministry, though he does not restrict his action to the acts of his ministers. They, for their part, must show their fidelity to God by serving their brethren as good stewards of the mysteries of God (cf. 1 Cor. 4. 1–2).

VI

THE ORDINATION OF MINISTERS FOR PASTORAL WORK

33. The pastoral ministry, because it expresses the apostolic

character of the Church, is conferred in the Christian community by the action of ministers already members of the apostolic community, signifying thereby the action of Christ, who is constantly sending servants of the gospel to his Church; that is what ordination means.

34. The risen Lord is he who calls to the ministry, ordains, and confers the gift. The ordination of ministers comprises the prayer asking for the gifts of the Holy Spirit and the laying on of hands which signifies them. It proclaims that the Church is bound up with the acts of Jesus Christ and his apostles.

35. The ordination of ministers is at once:
(a) an invocation to God to grant the gifts of the Holy Spirit for the needs of the ministry;
(b) the sacramental sign of the answering of this prayer by our Lord, who confers the necessary charisms;
(c) the welcome extended by the whole Church to the new servant and his reception into the college of ministers;
(d) the commitment of the minister to the ministry with which he is entrusted.

36. The ordained ministry is definitive in its fundamental reality of serving the gospel, the sacraments and the community. Its form may vary according to the needs of the Church and the mission entrusted to its ministers. The exercise of the pastoral ministry may be suspended for quite a long time without a new ordination being required if it is taken up again. Ordination, the sign of a difference of charisms between the pastoral ministry and the priesthood of the baptized, far from separating ministers from God's people and making them into a clerical caste, identifies them more fully with the life of the Church.

37. The foregoing text shows a fundamental agreement between us on the nature and significance of the pastoral ministry in the mystery of the Church. Difficulties remain, of which the chief seem to fall into two categories.

The first and most important lies in a different interpretation and appreciation of the concrete and historic shapes assumed by the apostolic succession in the ministry, owing to the separation of the churches.

The second derives from the great differences in the present organization and allocation of ministries on both sides.

These difficulties do not necessarily seem to us an obstacle to a future reconciliation of the ministries on the basis of the agreement reached.

Part Two
PROPOSAL FOR A RECOGNITION AND RECONCILIATION OF MINISTRIES

I
INTRODUCTION

38. The question of the ministries being a major obstacle to unity, it is on this point that the change of heart (*metanoia*) of the churches ought primarily to concentrate. We do not feel that a purely theological agreement can suffice to carry the churches the rest of the way towards unity. Our doctrinal agreement on the pastoral ministry already constitutes a reconciliation in faith; if it is accepted, the reconciliation will still need to be intimated by acts on the part of the churches. These might well create a new situation where problems relating to joint celebration would be solved because they would have ceased to exist. The reconciliation of the ministries would then take on a significant character in the eyes of our communities and of the world, in an effort to give the Church a new image.

39. Up to the present, a critical examination on each side, undertaken and accepted as a call to reform the Church, has enabled us to discern what, on our own side, is in conflict with our mutual beliefs about the ministry and what, on the other, is a sign and reminder of ecclesial value. We have been discovering in each other complementary virtues demanding to be practised in unity, for we have need one of another in order to be more perfectly the Church.

From now on, the efforts of the churches in the direction of conversion must tend toward and culminate in a word of mutual recognition, as well as in decisions in regard to themselves that will make possible an act of reconciliation of sacramental and ecclesial significance. Recognition and reconciliation each imply and call for the other.

The points on which a change of heart is necessary in order to achieve full reconciliation are the following:[16]

II
ON THE CATHOLIC SIDE

40. We propose that the substantial reality of the ministry that has emerged from the churches born of the Reformation be recognized; because of the defects and deviations that had come about in the exercise of the traditional ministries, and despite the shared sin of separation, God, ever faithful to his Church, gave these communities which continued living in an apostolic succession of faith a ministry of the word and sacraments, whose value is manifested by its fruits.[7] This ministry, which arose outside the episcopal succession, can in some cases claim to rest at least on the sign of a presbyteral succession.[8]

Consequently, to complete this recognition and give this ministry authority in the eyes of their people, the bishops would need to join it to the normal sign of the episcopal succession which is indispensable, in Catholic doctrine, to the fulness of the ministry perfectly signified. There is a necessary complementation between the mystery of the Church. They would thereby be affirming the necessary docility of the Church to the free initiatives of the Spirit.

41. We propose that a more collegial pattern be adopted for the exercise of the hierarchical ministry at universal and at local level, so as to show more visibly the ties of reciprocity that exist between the ministers and God's people and, similarly, between priests and bishops.

42. In this same spirit, we propose that more value be attached in the life of the Church to the various ministries or charisms founded on the priesthood of the laity and on Christian responsibility deriving from reception of baptism, confirmation, and the eucharist.

III
ON THE PROTESTANT SIDE

43. We propose that all the people of our churches should recognize the reality of a ministry of the word and of the sacraments in the Catholic Church. It would accordingly be for the authorities of our churches, on the basis of an agreement as to the nature of the ministry, to confer authority on Catholic ministers to minister to their people.

By reason of the situation created by the rupture in the sixteenth century, we recognize that we are deprived, not of the apostolic succession, but of the fulness of the sign of this succession. The result is a splintering off to form various national churches and the loss of the sense of the unity of the Church in time and in space. With a view to the unity of the Church and its ministries we recognize the necessity to return to the fulness of the sign of the apostolic succession.

44. We propose that a new value should be set on the significance of the 'episcopal' ministry, in particular in regard to its pastoral character, and that the sense of its personalization as a sign of unity should be revived.

45. We propose a review of the practice in certain Reformed churches of delegating authority to people who are not ordained to preach and to celebrate the Lord's supper, so that the difference in charisms between the ordained ministry and the priesthood of the laity shall no longer be obscured. We believe that the significance of ordination would be more clearly brought out by diversified ordinations.

46. On the basis of this mutual change of heart, the reconciliation of the ministries could take the form of a reciprocal laying on of hands,[9] a traditional apostolic gesture which expresses the action of Christ and of the Spirit in the visible body of the Church. Its several levels of meaning would enable it to signify a penitential act of reconciliation in which each side would recognize before the other where it was deficient and, at the same time, would be accompanied by the invocation of the Holy Spirit and directed towards a sending out into the world. It would give a wider and fuller investiture in the eyes of the churches concerned.

47. We are also aware that the reconciliation of the ministries we desire will pose in a more immediate fashion the question of the ministry of the unity of the universal Church. We propose to place this matter on our agenda for our coming meetings, if possible with the participation of our brothers of the Orthodox churches.

V

QUESTIONS

48. Might not the foregoing proposal contribute to a positive and ecclesially demanding solution of the urgent pastoral problems with which we are at present faced (certain chaplaincies, scattered communities, pastoral ministry to mixed households, ecumenical groups, etc.)? A reconciliation of ministries might be envisaged in certain cases where serious ecumenical work at pastoral and community level has brought to light a fundamental agreement in faith which makes it unequivocally possible. This might be done in the name of the legitimate initiative and discretion left to local churches.[10]

That is the spirit in which we have been working. We submit this question to the authorities of our respective churches.

PARTICIPANTS

ROMAN CATHOLIC	PROTESTANT
Père Jean-Noël Aletti	Pasteur Georges Appia
Père Paul Aymard	Pasteur Jacky Argaud
Père Joseph de Baciocchi	Pasteur Daniel Atger
Père René Beaupère	Pasteur André Benoit
Père Edmond Chavaz	Pasteur Alain Blancy
Père Marc Clément	Pasteur Henry Bruston
Père Irénée H. Dalmais	Pasteur Edouard Diserens
Père Jacques Desseaux	Pasteur M. Ferrier-Welti
Père André Fabre	Pasteur Jean Claud Ill
Père Claude Gerest	Pasteur Jean Jundt
Père René Girault	Pasteur Jean Kaltenmark
Père Etienne Goutagny	Pasteur Michel Leplay
Père Maurice Jourjon	Pasteur Louis Lévrier

ROMAN CATHOLIC (contd.)	PROTESTANT (contd.)
Père Marie Leblanc	Pasteur Marc Lods
Père Gustave Martelet	Pasteur Alain Martin
Père Pierre Michalon	Pasteur André Morel
Père André Perroux	Pasteur Hébert Roux
Père Jean Roche	Frère Max Thurian, of Taizé
Père Bernard Sesboué	Pasteur André Vermeil
Père Robert Stalder	Pasteur G. Westphal
Père Maurice Villain	

NOTES
PART ONE

1. *Vers une même foi eucharistique?* (Les Presses de Taizé 1972); ET, *Modern Eucharistic Agreement* (SPCK 1973), pp. 51–78.

2. Translator's note: All biblical quotations are taken from the Jerusalem Bible.

3. We shall henceforth designate as 'pastoral ministry', using this term in the strongest sense, the ministry whose foundation was described in paragraph 11 above and of which it is said that 'there is an apostolic succession in the ministry instituted by our Lord'. The term 'pastoral ministry' covers the whole variety of ordained ministries.

4. The term 'college' is not to be understood here in its legal or clerical sense but as the expression of 'ministerial communion'.

5. As regards the laying on of hands, which is practised to initiate true priests and ministers of the Church into their office, I have no objection to its being received as a sacrament 'for in it there is a ceremony first taken from Scripture, then one that Paul testifies not to be empty or superficial but a faithful token of spiritual grace (1 Tim. 4. 14). However, I have not put it as number three among the sacraments because it is not ordinary or common with all believers but is a special rite for a particular office' (Calvin, *Institutes* IV, XIX). Research still needs to be done on the subject of the sacramental nature of ordination, since this point looms large in ecumenical dialogue.

NOTES
PART TWO

6. They are formulated in the case of each confessional family in its own language.

7. Vatican II, *Decree on Ecumenism*, no. 3, 20–23.

8. By this we mean that Roman Catholic priests who went over to the Reformed churches ordained pastors. They were able to justify their action in doing so on the basis of one of the theological concepts of the day.
9. The laying on of hands should take place with the participation of officially qualified ministers.
10. By this is meant, on the Catholic side, the dioceses and, on the Protestant side, the ecclesiastical regions. To be legitimate, an initiative of this sort presupposes the obedience of each communion to its own discipline.

THE ORDAINED MINISTRY IN ECUMENICAL PERSPECTIVE

An agreed Statement of the Faith and Order Commission of the World Council of Churches

ACCRA 1974

© World Council of Churches 1974

The text here printed incorporates changes made at Accra in July 1974. This agreed statement is one of three published in *One Baptism, One Eucharist, and a Mutually Recognised Ministry*, Faith and Order Paper, No. 73, 1975

PREAMBLE

1. All ministry in the Church is to be understood in the light of him who came 'not to be served but to serve' (Mk 10. 45). It is he who said 'As my Father has sent me, even so I send you' (Jn 20. 21). Thus, our calling in Christ constrains us to a costly, dedicated, and humble involvement in the needs of mankind. Only so we may understand the whole ministry of the people of God, and only so the character of the special ministry of those who are called and set apart to serve and equip the Church by their stewardship of the mysteries of Christ.

I

THE ORDAINED MINISTRY AND THE CHRISTIAN COMMUNITY

2. The ordained ministry is to be understood as part of the community. An understanding of the ministry must therefore start from the nature of the Church, the community of believers. This conviction is now shared by most of the churches. Thus the following considerations start from the Christian community; they then try to define the nature and functions of the ordained ministry in the light of this community.

A. THE CHRISTIAN COMMUNITY

3. The Lord Jesus Christ, through his Word and Spirit, forgives sins and delivers men from the lordship of the powers of destruction; he continues to gather worshipping communities out of this broken world, the one people of God, coming from the water of baptism; he builds them up through Word and Sacrament.

4. Membership in the community of the Church involves fellowship with God the Father through Jesus Christ, in the Holy Spirit; it means being in a relationship of mutual indwelling with

Jesus Christ. This fellowship makes possible a unique experience of community, based as it is upon communion with God and repentance, upon mutual forgiveness and acceptance; it results in freedom and new life. God's purpose is that all men should be brought into this community.

5. Among the marks of this community, apostolicity has a central place for the understanding of the ministry. Christ is the true apostle whom God, in the Holy Spirit, sent into the world. Through him the world is reconciled to the Father in the communion of the Holy Spirit. The apostles whom Christ chose and sent to continue this mission of reconciliation, are the foundations of the community created by the Spirit. To this community Christ gave the authority to accomplish the apostolic mission. The Holy Spirit realizes this mission by communicating and manifesting himself in this community.

6. The apostolicity of the Church is thus rooted in Christ's mission and inseparably bound to the fullness of the witness and service of the apostles. The Christian community must constantly strive to be faithful to this witness and service, yet its apostolicity is sustained primarily by Christ's continued presence in it through the activity of the Holy Spirit.

7. The Christian community always exists in a concrete sociological setting. Therefore, it cannot be described adequately in general theological terms. As we reflect on the nature of the community and on the place of the special ministry in the community its actual sociological appearance must be taken into account. Obviously, the forms of the community have changed in the course of history; and as the special ministry is to serve the community in its concrete form, the patterns of the ministry have changed and must change as well.

8. In the twentieth century, for example, geographical areas no longer delineate certain social entities as they once did. Urbanization and the modern organization of society continue to develop; owing to the characteristic mobility, dispersal and specialization of this society, persons tend to belong to several communities simultaneously, no one of which is primarily geo-

graphically defined. This development is tending more and more to be true of continuing 'rural' societies as well.[1]

9. No doubt the traditional groups of people and pastor in a relatively homogeneous neighbourhood, where such exist and are authentic, will continue to be important and living expressions of the Church. In our day, however, Christian people have membership in a number of diverse communities, outside as well as inside the Christian fellowship. The great mobility characteristic of our time makes possible many new groupings of Christians on non-geographic bases. Many fruitful ministries are emerging in such new communities.

10. Christ sends his Church into the world to participate in his ministry of reconciliation and liberation, and membership in these diverse communities forces many pressing human concerns into the centre of the Christian fellowship. The Church should take the needs, worries, and hopes of its surrounding culture seriously; these can become the concern of the whole of the Christian fellowship. The daily scattering of disciples throughout this variety of communities provides new opportunities for them to participate in movements of human fulfilment, liberation, 'consciousness-raising', and service. Through these groups too Christ is building up his kingdom in the hearts of men 'to unite all things in him'.

B. THE MINISTRY OF THE WHOLE PEOPLE OF GOD

11. The Church as the communion of the Holy Spirit is called to proclaim and prefigure the Kingdom of God by announcing the gospel to the world and by being built up as the body of Christ. Within these two commissions each member of the body is called to live his faith and account for his hope. Each stands alongside men and women in their joy and suffering and witnesses among them through loving service; each struggles with the oppressed toward that freedom and dignity promised with the coming of the Kingdom.

12. This proclamation of the gospel, service to the world, and edification of the community require a variety of activities, both permanent and provisional, spontaneous and institutional. To

fulfil these needs the Holy Spirit gives diverse and complementary gifts to the Church. These gifts are given by God to individuals for the common good of his people and their service and manifest themselves in acts of service within the Christian community and to the world. They are all gifts of the same Spirit. The ordained ministry, therefore, cannot be understood or carried out in isolation from the general ministry of the whole people.

C. THE BASIS AND FUNCTION OF THE ORDAINED MINISTRY

13. In order that his redemptive work might be proclaimed and attested to the ends of the earth, and that its fruits might be communicated to man, Christ chose apostles and committed to them the word of reconciliation.[2] Within the first Christian communities the apostles exercised a unique and fundamental function, which could not be handed on. However, insofar as they bore special (but not exclusive) responsibility for proclaiming the message of reconciliation, establishing churches and building them up in the apostolic faith, their ministry had to be continued. Although there was a variety of gifts in the early Church, the New Testament reports a setting apart to special ministry, distinctions of service were made.[3] This special ministry was essential then; it is essential in all times and circumstances. Such a ministry is exercised by persons who are called within the community and given gifts and authority to transmit the living testimony of the apostles.

14. Christ, through the Holy Spirit, stirs up, strengthens, and sends those whom he has called for this special ministry, making them ambassadors of his message and work. Persons called to this ministry are commissioned to serve the work of the Lord by following him, being conformed to him and by announcing his name. The presence of this ministry in the community signifies the priority of divine initiative and authority in the Church's existence. Thus, whatever the diversity of functions in a Christian community may be, the specific service of the ordained minister is to assemble the community and to serve it by pointing to its fundamental dependence on Jesus Christ—Christ who is the source of its mission and the foundation of its unity.

15. *The essential and specific function of the special ministry is: to assemble and build up the Christian community, by proclaiming and teaching the word of God, and presiding over the liturgical and sacramental life of the eucharistic community.* The Christian community and the special ministry are related to one another. The minister cannot exist and fulfil his task in isolation. He needs the support and encouragement of the community. On the other hand, the Christian community needs the special ministry which serves to co-ordinate and unite the different gifts in the community and to strengthen and enable the ministry of the whole People of God. But above all, this relationship and mutual dependence manifests that the Church is not master of the Word and Sacrament, nor the source of its faith, hope and unity. Christian life as well as the ministry are received from the living Christ in the Church.

16. The setting apart by God for this special ministry requires from the side of the Church a recognition of which a form is already found in apostolic times (cf. e.g., 2 Tim. 1. 6–7) and which later became commonly known as ordination.

D. MINISTRY AND AUTHORITY

17. The setting apart for this special ministry implies both consecration to service and authority for its exercise. Since all ministry is rooted in that of Christ, its essential quality is seen in such words as these: 'I am among you as one who serves' (Luke 22. 24). The commission which Christ gave his apostles is set in this light in such a passage as John 17. 18–26 and is so accepted by St Paul who exalts his ministry as an apostle in terms of a sharing in the suffering of Christ: 'Always bearing in the body the death of Jesus so that the life of Jesus may also be manifested in our bodies' (2 Cor. 4. 10).

18. The exercise of such ministry has authority which ultimately belongs to Christ who has received it from the Father (Matt. 28. 18); it is in this sense a divine authority. On the other hand, since ordination is essentially a setting apart with prayer for the gifts of the Holy Spirit for the continuing constitution and edification of the body, the authority of the ordained ministry is not

to be understood as an individual possession of the ordained person but belongs to the whole community in and for which the minister is ordained. Authority in the name of God in its exercise must involve the participation of the whole community. The ordained minister manifests and exercises the authority of Christ in the way Christ himself revealed God's authority to the world: in and through *communion*.

19. This in practice means that the ordained ministry is authoritative only in and through the concrete community to which it belongs. The ordained minister is *not* an autocrat nor an impersonal functionary. He is bound to the faithful in interdependence and reciprocity, although his role is one of responsible leadership and judgement. Only if the authority of the ordained minister finds genuine acknowledgement in the communion of the community can this authority be protected from the distortion of domination.

E. MINISTRY AND PRIESTHOOD

20. Even if the New Testament never uses the terms '*priest-hiereus*' or '*priesthood-hierateuma*' to designate the ordained minister or the ministry, tradition has not been afraid of this usage. Although churches emerging from the Reformation avoid the word priesthood to designate the ordained ministry, churches of the Catholic tradition employ this word in diverse forms: priestly ministry, ministerial priesthood, or, more recently, ministry of priesthood. The search for a reconciliation in ministries makes it especially useful to discuss this question of terms.

21. This manner of expression always refers the function of the priests to a priestly reality upon which theirs is based, but which exceeds it: that is, the unique priesthood of Christ and the royal and prophetic, common and universal priesthood of the baptized (1 Pet. 2. 9; Rev. 1. 6; 3. 10; 20. 6). The priesthood of Christ and the priesthood of the baptized community is a function of sacrifice and intercession. As Christ offers himself for all men, the Christian offers his whole being 'as a living sacrifice' (Rom. 12. 1). As Christ intercedes to the Father for all men, the Christian prays for the liberation of his human brothers. The minister, who

participates, as every Christian, in the priesthood of Christ, and of all the People of God, fulfils his particular priestly service in strengthening, building up, and expressing the royal and prophetic priesthood of the faithful through the service of the gospel, the leading of the liturgical and sacramental life of the eucharistic community, and intercession.

22. The ordained ministry is then of a completely new and different nature in relation to the sacrificial priesthood of the Old Testament. As he offers his life for the service of the mission in the world and of the edification of the Church, the minister is, as St Paul says about himself, 'a minister of Jesus Christ to the Gentiles in the priestly service of the gospel of God, so that the offering of the Gentiles may be acceptable, sanctified by the Holy Spirit' (Rom. 15. 16).

F. THE DIVERSITY OF MINISTRY

23. So far the discussion has concerned the one ordained ministry, which can be discerned in various churches in various forms and structures. The form which ordained ministry takes in any church tradition is due to the interaction of three elements: (1) The givenness of the commission of Jesus and the reception of the Spirit; (2) The changing patterns of society; (3) The Church's response in the Spirit to those changing patterns in the social environment.

24. When the diversity of ordained ministry among the various churches is examined, it is evident that this diversity is bound up with the history and cultural particularity of those churches. Each case reveals what might be called a particular 'theological-ecclesial culture', i.e. a coherence of theology, piety, liturgical tradition, community life, geographical origin, law, and jurisprudence. So the diversity of ministerial structures is part of a more complex ecclesial diversity of styles and types, reflecting weighty differences of a theological, sociological, and psychological nature. But the limits of ministerial diversity are determined by the apostolic commission, the action of the Holy Spirit, and the fact that major patterns of leadership in society are not infinitely variable.

25. The plurality of ecclesial cultures and ministerial structures does not diminish the one ministerial reality found in Christ and constituted by the Holy Spirit in the commission of the Apostles. Among the various ministerial structures the threefold ministry of bishop, presbyter-priest, and deacon predominates. But it would be wrong to exclude other patterns of ministry which are found among the churches. Within the same community of faith it is possible to have, side by side, various styles of ecclesial life and ministerial structures, without making the one the model for all the others.

26. There is unity in the diversity of ministerial structures, in that the essential elements of ministry can always be identified in the very plurality and multiformity of ecclesial styles and structures. It would be difficult to imagine any structure of ministry which did not incorporate *episcope*, as that oversight of the Church and of the celebration of the Christian mystery which belongs to the gospel, and *presbyteral* function understood as the proclamation of the gospel and administration of the sacraments. Both the episcopal and presbyteral functions of the Church must be understood as a sharing in the *diakonia*, that is, as costly service to the community of the Church and to the world through the proclamation and actualization of the gospel. In the course of history, the function of *diakonia* has found expression in the office of deacon and the deaconess. For about twenty years now, many churches, independently from one another, have been giving attention to the possible renewal of this office.

II

APOSTOLIC SUCCESSION

27. The primary manifestation of apostolic succession is to be found in the life of the Church as a whole. This succession is an expression of the permanence and, therefore, continuity of Christ's own mission in which the Church partakes. This participation is rooted in the gift of the Holy Spirit in the sending of the apostles and their successors, and will find its completion in the all-embracing realization of God's kingdom.

28. The fullness of the apostolic succession of the whole Church involves continuity in the permanent characteristics of the Church of the apostles: witness to the apostolic faith, proclamation and fresh interpretation of the apostolic gospel, transmission of ministerial responsibility, sacramental life, community in love, service for the needy, unity among local churches, and sharing the gifts which the Lord has given to each.

29. The ordained ministry is related in various degrees to all of these characteristics. It serves as an authorized and responsible instrument for their preservation and actualization. The orderly transmission of the ministry is, therefore, both a visible sign of the continuity of the whole Church and of the effective participation of the ministry in it and contribution to it. Where this orderly transmission is lacking, a church must ask itself whether its apostolicity can be maintained in its fullness. Or, where this ministry does not adequately subserve the Church's apostolicity, a church must ask itself whether or not its ministerial structures should continue with no alteration.

30. Under the particular historical circumstance of the growing Church in the sub-apostolic age, the succession of bishops became one of the ways in which the apostolicity of the Church was expressed. This succession was understood as serving, symbolizing, and guarding the continuity of the apostolic faith and communion. Some Christian traditions believe this faith and communion to have been preserved uniquely in this form of ministerial succession, even though there have been varying interpretations and understandings of this succession among these same traditions.

31. Today there is growing agreement among scholars that the New Testament presents diverse types of organization of the Christian communities, according to the difference of authors, places, and times. While, in the local churches, founded by apostles like Paul, there were persons in authority, very little is said about how they were appointed and about the requirements for presiding at the eucharist. On this basis, there have been developed, in the course of history, notably since the sixteenth century,

multiple forms of church order, each with its own advantages and disadvantages: episcopal, presbyteral, congregational, among others.

32. There is further agreement among many scholars that although ordination of ministers by bishops was the almost universal practice in the Church very early, it is impossible to show that such a church order existed everywhere in the Church from the earliest times. In fact, there is evidence that in the subapostolic age even this practice did not become uniform until after some time. Further, there have been well-documented cases in the history of the Western Church in which priests, not bishops, have, with papal dispensation, ordained other priests to serve at the altar.

33. These observations do not imply a devaluation of the emergence and general acceptance of the historic episcopate. They only indicate that the Church has been able to respond to the needs of particular historical situations in the development of its ministerial structures. It follows, therefore, that faithfulness to the basic task and structure of the apostolic ministry can be combined with an openness to diverse and complementary expressions of this apostolic ministry. Such insights, together with a more comprehensive understanding of the apostolicity of the Church and the means of its preservation and actualization, have led to certain modifications of previously held positions:

34. (1) A growing tendency is noticeable among theologians in certain churches which have preserved the historic episcopate to interpret episcopal succession as an effective sign, not a guarantee, of the continuity of the Church in apostolic faith and mission, which is manifested in doctrine, proclamation, sacraments, worship, life, and service. They value the succession of ministries that have the fullness of *episcope* as a gift of God, which they must preserve.

35. (2) Many find it possible today to recognize a continuity in apostolic faith, mission, and ministry in churches which have not retained the form of historic episcopacy. This recognition finds additional support in the fact that the episcopal functions and

reality have been preserved in many of these churches, with or without the title 'bishop'. Ordination, for example, is always done in them by persons in whom the church recognizes the authority to transmit ministerial commission.

36. (3) Many are also increasingly aware of the fact that the traditional ways of transmitting ministerial commission, whether in churches with episcopal structures or not, are not necessarily exhaustive. In particular situations, e.g., a ministry may emerge which, because of its authority, is accepted by the particular community and receives only afterwards a form of official recognition. Or, in other situations, new forms of ministry are raised by the Holy Spirit. In responding to these ministries the Church should not quench the Spirit, but rather welcome them as an enrichment of its life and service.

37. The importance of the historic episcopate has not been diminished by the above-mentioned findings. On the contrary, these new insights are enabling churches without the historic episcopate to appreciate it as a sign of the continuity and unity of the Church. More and more churches, including those in church union negotiations, are expressing willingness to see episcopacy as a pre-eminent sign of the apostolic succession of the whole Church in faith, life, and doctrine, and as such, something that ought to be striven for if absent. The only thing they hold as incompatible with contemporary historical and theological research is the notion that the episcopal succession is identical with and comprehends the apostolicity of the whole Church.

III

ORDINATION

A. THE MEANING OF ORDINATION

38. The Church, in ordaining some of its members to the ministry in the name of Christ, attempts to follow the mission of the Apostles and to remain faithful to their teaching. Ordination as an act attests the bond of the Church with Jesus Christ and the apostolic witness, recalling that it is the risen Lord who is the true

ordainer, who bestows the gift. In ordaining, the Church provides, under the inspiration of the Holy Spirit, for the faithful proclamation of the Gospel and humble service in Christ's name. The laying-on of hands can be seen as the sign of the gift of the Spirit, rendering visible the ordering of this ministry in the revelation accomplished in him, and reminding the Church to look to him as the source of its commission.[4]

39. Properly speaking, then, ordination denotes an action by God and by the community which inaugurates a relationship in which the ordained is strengthened by the Spirit for his or her task and is upheld by the acknowledgement and prayers of the congregation.

40. This basic understanding has been elaborated both theologically and liturgically in many different ways. It becomes increasingly important in ecumenical discussion to seek to understand how this process of elaboration occurs and to take full account of its consequences. Beyond their etymologies and dictionary definitions, words become the carriers of implicit metaphors, the vehicle of unconscious assumptions about human relationships and the functioning of social institutions derived from the cultures of different times and places. The taken-for-granted background of a given term often has its hidden influence on the way that term is combined with others to form more complex structures of thought. The same is true of the combination of symbolic acts to form liturgies.

41. Extensive study has already been devoted to the contexts and meanings of the Hebrew, Greek, and Latin words connected with ordination.[4] It is evident that there is considerable difference between the unspoken cultural setting of the Greek *cheirotonein* and that of the Latin *ordo* or *ordinare*. The New Testament use of the former term borrows its basic secular meaning of 'appointment' (Acts 14. 23; 2 Cor. 8. 19), which is, in turn, derived from the original meaning of extending the hand, either to designate a person or to cast a vote. Some scholars see in *cheirotonein* a reference to the act of laying on hands, in view of the literal description of such action in such seemingly parallel instances as Acts 6. 6;

8. 17; 18. 19; 13. 3; 19. 6; 1 Tim. 4. 14; 2 Tim. 1. 6. But the actual use of *cheirotonein* need mean no more than 'appoint' without reference either to the theory or means of the action. *Ordo* and *ordinare*, on the other hand, are terms derived from Roman law where they convey the notion of the special status of a group distinct from the plebs, as in the term *ordo clarissimus* for the Roman senate. The starting point of any conceptual construction using these terms will strongly influence what is taken for granted in both the thought and action which result.

42. Similar analyses could well be made of the social metaphors underlying many other terms employed in this discussion: 'clergy' and 'laity', 'minister', 'episcopos', 'deacon'. It is appropriate, of course, to think of God's use of man's metaphors as no less sacramental than his use of such products of human labour as bread and wine. The work of grace is present 'in, with, and through' both language and social conventions. But at the same time, it is important to be aware of the way unconscious assumptions of this nature may condition theological argument. Social metaphors are inevitable if we believe God has entered our social history, which theology and liturgy seek to represent.

43. The original New Testament terms for ordination tend to be simple and descriptive. The fact of appointment is recorded. The laying on of hands is described. There seems to be no warrant for building any particular theory—whether 'Catholic' or 'Protestant'—on the New Testament evidence alone. Thus when the theory and practice of ordination are worked out, as they must be, to meet new conditions and opportunities, care must be taken to be aware of the intellectual process involved. Ecumenical dialogue may well include a mutual effort to uncover the implicit, the unconscious, the unspoken dimensions of what we think and do. Such effort could both break down barriers and enhance our appreciation of the symbolic and experiential riches we have in common.

B. THE ACT OF ORDINATION

44. The act of ordination is at one and the same time: invocation

of the Holy Spirit (*epiclesis*); sacramental sign; acknowledgement of gifts and commitment.

It is:

45. (1) An invocation to God that he bestow the power of the Holy Spirit upon the new minister in his new relation to the local Christian community, to the Church universal, and to the world. The otherness of God's initiative, of which the ordained ministry is a symbol, is here acknowledged in the act of ordination itself. 'The Spirit blows where it wills' (John 3. 3), and invocation of the Spirit implies an absolute dependence on God for the outcome of the Church's prayer. This means that the Spirit may set new forces in motion and open new possibilities 'far more abundantly than all that we ask or think' (Eph. 3. 20).

46. (2) A sign of the granting of this prayer by the Lord who gives the gift of ministry. Although the outcome of the Church's epiclesis depends on the freedom of God, the Church ordains in confidence that God, being faithful to his promise in Christ, enters sacramentally into contingent, historical forms of human relationship and uses them for his purpose. Ordination is a sign performed in faith that the spiritual relationship signified is present in, with, and through the words spoken, the gestures made and the ecclesiastical forms employed.

47. (3) An acknowledgement by the Church of its discernment of gifts of the Spirit in the one ordained, and a commitment by both Church and ordinand, to the tests and opportunities implied in the new relationship. By receiving the new minister in the act of ordination, the congregation acknowledges this minister's gifts and commits itself to responsibility for an openness toward him. Likewise the one ordained offers his gifts to the Church and commits himself to the burden and opportunity of new authority and responsibility.

48. In order to experience and demonstrate the truth that setting apart is not to some superior level of discipleship, but rather to service within the Church, it is important that the entire process of ordination involve the whole body of the people. There needs to be continual emphasis on the fact that ordination is not only

'over against' nor *vis-à-vis* the congregation, but rather, that a person is addressed in the midst of the people. It is also important that the congregation have a part in the calling, choosing and training of an ordinand, preserving the basic significance of the call to the ministry. This means more than the inclusion of a sentence or two in the liturgy and ordaining in the presence of the laity, important as that may be.[5]

49. A long and early Christian tradition places ordination in the context of worship and especially of the eucharist. Such a place for the service of ordination preserves the understanding of ordination as an *act* of the *whole* community, and not of a certain order within it or of the individual ordained. Even if one believes that the act of ordaining belongs to a special order within the Church, it is always important to remember that the entire community is involved in the act. Ordination, in association with the eucharist, keeps before the Church the truth that it is an act which initiates a person to a *service of the 'koinonia'*, (the fellowship), a service both to God and to the fellow man. It is this *koinonia* that the eucharist expresses *par excellence* and by continuing to relate ordination to the eucharist this dimension of ministry is called to mind. Ordination within the service of the eucharist also reminds the Church that the ordained ministry is set apart to point to Christ's own ministry and not to some other. By placing ordination in the context of worship and especially the eucharist, this act is referred to God himself and the ordained person is dedicated to the service of 'his Servant' who offers himself for the salvation of the world.[6]

C. CONDITIONS FOR ORDINATION

50. It follows from what has been said about ordination that certain pre-conditions and expectations regarding the ordinand are indispensable, while others are not. It is especially important today to be clear about this in view of the multitude of experiments in new forms of ministry with which the churches are approaching the modern world. Among the basic requirements the following points seem worthy of consideration:

51. (1) The ordinand should be one who has a call from the Lord

to dedicate himself to the particular style of ministry implied in ordination. This call will be discerned by the ordinand himself, by the Christian community, and by its spiritual leaders. It is discerned through personal prayer and reflection, as well as through suggestion, example, encouragement, guidance coming from family, friends, teachers, the school, the congregation, the seminary. It will be tested and fostered and confirmed or perhaps modified particularly through the years of training.

52. (2) The ordinand should be one whom the Church can confidently expect to commit himself to the task for which he is called and ordained. This task has to bear a clear relation to the Church's mission, however innovative the proposed patterns of activity. It will largely consist in gathering and building up some form of missioning Christian Community, and in aiding thereby and enabling members of the community to exercise ever more fully their own ministry, each in his or her respective sphere of activity.

52. (3) The ordinand should be one capable of carrying out the ministry in informed fidelity to the gospel of Christ and to Christ's lordship over the actual situation within which the service is rendered. He should be able to read and discern the signs of the times. He should, therefore, be appropriately prepared through adequate study of Scripture and theology, and through sufficient acquaintance with the social and human realities of the actual situation.

54. (4) The ordinand, regardless of the type and mode of his professional activity, should be one endowed with such basic gifts of the Spirit as faithfulness and reliability, prayerfulness and patience, endurance, courage, humility, and hope. He is called to be, weak, foolish, and sinful though he is, the sign of God's invitation to forgiveness and repentance. His ministry is often better fulfilled by quiet listening and continued searching than by many words and strong assertions.

55. (5) The ordinand should be one who, in fulfilling his appointed task as ordained minister, will be able to live and act in a relationship of mutual accountability and concern, both within the People

of God and among his or her brothers and sisters who have also been called to ministries.

56. These are some of the conditions which seem to be indispensable for ordination. Other conditions, traditionally considered necessary, may have to be rethought and modified as called for by changing situations and new forms of ministry:

57. (a) Both celibacy and marriage are vocations from God and gifts of the Spirit. Either of these can be used by God to bless the ordained minister and enrich his ministry.

58. (b) The academic programme should be flexible and considerable elasticity is to be admitted in requirements regarding degrees. To be sure, the ordained minister requires a competence suitable to the style of ministry to be undertaken and calls for the intellectual training necessary to understand the questions men around are asking and to search along with them for theological answers. It does not, however, follow that such competence and training are achieved only through formal study or the acquisition of degrees or prescribed patterns of formation. The variety of situations and of groups to be served demands various types of preparation for the ministry. Team ministries, in particular, will find their capacity to serve greatly enhanced by diversified formation. What is said here is in no way intended to diminish the importance to the Church of its doctors of theology, its trained interpreters of Scriptures, or its experts in other disciplines. It is intended, rather, to emphasize the truth that certain kinds of ministry may need other competences even more, including extensive experience in the 'secular' world.

59. (c) Ministries need not always be salaried from church sources. Financial support from the Church is not essential to ordained ministry and may, in cases, even diminish its effectiveness. While the Church has a clear duty to make financial provision for its servants, support may come from other sources, not excluding work done by the minister himself, providing this remains subordinate to and serves the purpose for which he was ordained. This possibility is often described as a 'tent-making' ministry, following the example of St Paul.

60. (d) The exercise of ministry could be full-time or part-time; both possibilities should be accepted. Nothing in Scripture demands that all ministers be full-time and employed by the Church. Full-time ministry has advantages and may be indispensable in some situations. There are, however, other circumstances in which part-time arrangements for ministerial leadership are possible and helpful. The secular experience of the minister, which is implied in these arrangements, could enrich the ministry and the minister's work in the secular world could commend the gospel. On the other hand, the new problems which can arise for a minister in secular employment require sympathetic study.

61. (e) While a good many will be ordained for service within the Church's visible organization, the possibility of ordination for the Church's ministry of word and sacrament outside this organization must always remain open. Such ordained persons might then live as bricklayers, as industrial managers, or as TV scriptwriters, for example.

62. (f) While the initial commitment to ordained ministry ought normally to be made without reserve or time limit, leave of absence from service is not incompatible with ordination and should be granted on reasonable grounds. There may also be cases in which an ordained minister wishes to relinquish exercise of his special ministry; a request made for serious reasons to relinquish it should be granted without opprobrium or reproach. Such a procedure need not mean in every case that the minister's service was not blessed by the Holy Spirit, or that the initial act of ordination was a mistake, or that one's status as an ordained person and the special relationship to the community constituted by ordination ceases to exist. Resumption of ministry will require no reordination.

63. In conclusion, it is important to remember that all ministries, old or new, for which men and women are ordained and in which they are engaged, be regarded by the Church as of equal importance and with equal rights. Neither parish ministries nor experimental or specialized ministries should be allowed to have prestige in the Church at the expense of the other.

D. THE ORDINATION OF WOMEN

64. Both men and women need to discover the full meaning of their specific contribution to the ministry of Christ. The Church is entitled to the style of ministry which can be provided by women as well as that which can be provided by men. Indeed, an understanding of our mutual interdependence needs to be more widely reflected in all branches of ministry. If ministry demands the engagement of the full humanity of those involved in it, may it not also be enriched by the creative interaction of men and women in relationship?

65. Since those who advocate the ordination of women do so out of their understanding of the meaning of the gospel and ordination, and since the experience of the churches in which women are ordained has on the whole been positive and none has found reason to reconsider its decision, the question must be asked as to whether it is not time for all the churches to confront this matter forthrightly. Churches which ordain women have found that women's gifts are as wide and varied as men's, and that their ministry is as fully blessed by the Holy Spirit as the ministry of men. The force of nineteen centuries of tradition against the ordination of women cannot be lightly ignored. It cannot be dismissed as lack of respect for the role of women in the Church. It raises theological as well as sociological questions which must be faced.[7] The discussion of these questions within several churches and Christian traditions should be complemented by joint study and reflection within the ecumenical fellowship of all churches.

66. It seems clear that, without repudiating the efficacy of their ministries in the past, many churches are reading passages such as Genesis 1. 27 and Galatians 3. 28 with a sensitivity arising from new circumstances and new needs. The implications for the ordained ministry both of the relatedness of men and women as created in the image of God and of the transcending of the distinction between them in the perspective of redemption in Christ, need to be more fully explored. The different traditions read the same facts in different ways. Without denying the relatedness of the sexes in either creation or redemption, churches which ordain

men only tend to see sexual differentiation as requiring a clearly defined separation of social roles. Churches which ordain both men and women, on the other hand, may risk the danger of underestimating the anthropological and social significance of difference between the sexes.

67. Theological reasoning and church practice on both sides of this debate may be adversely influenced by continuing the predominance of male imagery in the modern social and cultural context. Although contemporary society, particularly in the West, affords greater equality to women than the society of biblical times, both proponents and opponents of the ordination of women are subject to assumptions of male dominance which are part of the fabric of language and custom. Such taken-for-granted conceptual patterns may distort theological reasoning and institutional practice both in churches which ordain women and in those which do not.

68. The feeling of some men that their security and authority are challenged is a real but theologically subsidiary issue in this matter. So is the frustration that some women feel as they seek greater power and influence in society. The Church must minister in full awareness of social and psychological factors both to those who feel threatened and to those who feel frustrated, taking the side of freedom, justice, and truth where those can be discerned. But the question of who may be ordained, related as it is to this issue, is not the same question. The patterns of ministry are shaped by the Church in obedience to its understanding of the gospel, as interpreted by the Spirit in an ever-changing contemporary situation. It is on these grounds that the question of ordination should be judged.

69. For some churches these problems are not yet alive. While recording a position, they have not yet determined whether the decisive factors are doctrinal or simply related to a long-standing traditional discipline. Nor are individuals within the different confessions in agreement about the doctrinal and disciplinary factors or about their relation. Differences on this issue could raise

possible obstacles to the mutual recognition of ministries. But these obstacles should not be regarded as insuperable. Openness to each other holds out the possibility that the Spirit may well speak to one church through the insights of another. Ecumenical awareness and responsibility also demand that once a church has decided what is timely and right, it should act in obedience to its own conviction. Since the opinion appears to be growing that doctrinal considerations either favour the ordination of women or are neutral, the possibility is open that a future ecumenical council might deal with the question. Ecumenical considerations, therefore, should encourage, not restrain, the full, frank facing of this question.

IV

THE MINISTRY IN PRACTICE TODAY

A. CHANGE AND RENEWAL IN CHURCH AND MINISTRY

70. The Church is the people of God in history. It is part of the world to which it is sent. As human society changes, the Church is called to seek a new obedience to God in the new situation. For instance, if in society new means of communication are developed, they will have their effect upon the ministry of the Word. For example, if in a society there is a great movement of population from countryside to city, a church whose structures are wholly adapted to a rural situation is challenged to change them. Such manifestation is required in order that the Church may do in the world what it exists to do: which is, by the power of Christ, to proclaim and show in its own life the breaking in of the Kingdom.

71. In our time the world in which the Church of God finds itself is undergoing bewilderingly rapid change. The Church must therefore renew its efforts to adapt its mission and life. Its capacity for change is a measure of the vitality of the Church and its ministry. The response of a church to the changing situations in the world must combine the resources which God has imparted to his pilgrim people in the past with the insight that they receive from the world in which God has placed them.[8]

B. THE ROLE OF THE MINISTER

72. An essential element of the renewal of the Church is the renewal of the ministry. Any doctrine of the ministry conveys the image of a role which the minister has to fulfil in the Christian community. As he accepts the ministry he approaches the congregation with his own understanding of his task. He will soon discover, however, that the actual expectations of the Christian community differ from his own understanding. He needs to take these expectations into account.

73. Ministers experiencing such tension face a difficult dilemma. Either they adhere to their vision of the ordained ministry and alienate the congregation, or they adjust to the role they are actually expected to play and experience feelings of guilt.

74. In many situations the discrepancy between the minister's understanding of his role and the expectations which his congregation may have, conceals deeper tensions of which neither may be fully aware. Thus the Christian community may actually want of their minister something substantially different from what they say they want. Again what the minister in fact does may be different from what he thinks he is doing.

75. A precondition of renewal may be that ministers and congregation together should seek greater honesty about the conflicts in the situation and be ready to bear the tension creatively. Both the minister and the Christian community must ask in what ways their expectations need correction. The outcome may be radical change and the total or partial abandonment of traditional patterns. A serious problem faces the minister who wishes to transform the Church in an attempt to respond to the challenge of the coming Kingdom of God but whom the institutional Church, that has ordained and supports him, expects to devote his ministry chiefly to producing statistically measurable results or to keeping a church plant in repair.

76. A particular difficulty arises in the case of ministry to a congregation which combines loyalty to the Christian gospel with loyalties of a political and cultural kind. e.g. Northern Ireland

or South Africa). Alternatively, a congregation may be confronted by a minister whose view of his role contains political and social implications which the congregation cannot accept. (This too might be illustrated from Northern Ireland or South Africa.)

77. Increasingly, many ordained ministers have had to determine for themselves how closely they may or can ally themselves with reformatory or revolutionary movements. They have had to do this in the tormenting awareness that the initial and praiseworthy purpose of these movements was to right injustices and to reform dehumanizing social and political structures, but their progress has sometimes disclosed that they may have within themselves the seeds of other injustices and of other dehumanizing structures.

78. This conflict between different understandings of the role of the minister is a challenge to the minister's authority as well as to the mutual responsibility of the minister and the congregation in relation to each other. As all ministerial authority ultimately belongs to Christ, and the essential quality of all ministry is to be service, the minister has to ask himself how far he is justified in insisting upon his position over against the congregation by referring to his ordination. The congregation has to ask itself how far there are limits to its reponse to the authority of the minister; but above all, both parties have to look at their disagreements in light of Christ's commission to his Church as a whole and their mutual responsibility to the will of Christ as well as to each other.

C. NEW MINISTRIES AND OLD MINISTRIES

79. The experience of God's pilgrim people in both the remote and the recent past makes it clear that new forms of ministry may turn out to have as much to recommend them as the forms that a church in a given time or place may have inherited. At the same time, patterns of the ministry with a long history in the Church frequently have proved to be eminently adaptable to new situations. A church in a given time and place ought not, therefore, lightly to abandon an inherited pattern or replace it with a different arrangement merely because the inherited pattern is old and the different arrangement is new. For that reason, a church today may indeed find it possible and even highly desirable to retain or

take over a venerable and traditional pattern of the ordained ministry—for example, the inherited parish ministry—as long as this pattern shows itself capable of accommodation to the needs of a new situation that a given church confronts. At the same time, a church should not be faulted if it supplements an inherited pattern with new forms, or if it reacts to the problems raised by a new social situation by devising new and experimental ministries. For example, ministries to members of specific professions and occupational groupings have filled vital needs in many places. At any rate, in the allowing of new forms of ministry, the churches have paradigms in the multiformity of the ministry in the apostolic and sub-apostolic Church as the New Testament reflects it, as well as in subsequent periods and in other places in the Church's long history.

80. The need for a sharpened sense of ecumenical responsibility at this point cannot be overstressed. The interrelatedness of the churches that has made the modern Ecumenical Movement both possible and necessary should have made us all aware that no church can wholly escape the impact of another church's action. It may not always be possible to implement changes in the structures of ministry through an ecumenical forum, desirable as this may be. Indeed, certain problems, even certain almost universal problems, may be amenable to solution only at a denominational or even local level. But in the process of making changes each church should seek to be as sensitive as possible to the potential ecumenical implications of its solutions to its problems, especially in so sensitive an area as the ministry.

81. Furthermore, it is important that the devising and assessing of new and experimental forms of ministry should not be in the hands of ordained ministers alone, but that at every stage the opinion and experience of lay people should be listened to, and allowed to count in decision-making.

82. Many situations now require a team ministry made up of ordained ministers from different churches. For example, a university chaplaincy, counselling or hospital chaplaincy, or a team ministry to a church may naturally be served in this way.

83. (1) Experience shows that such an enterprise brings into the open some of the deep contrasts between the different ecclesial traditions of ministry, in 'image' or 'personal' formation. Two churches may have clear theological agreement about the eucharist but the minister of the one may be shaped by a tradition of daily liturgy and communion in church which the minister of the other would find strange. In a team ministry contrasts of this kind have to be faced, contained, and worked through, as more generally in the development of closer ecumenical co-operation between churches.

84. (2) In any case the combined ministry of an ecumenical team (say, on a university campus) cannot but be a powerful instrument for the education of the laity of the Church. A Christian brought up within one ecclesial tradition is confronted by a wide range of style in both worship and ministry and by the emergence of new styles. Such an experience is bound to create the possibility of new insights into the meaning of the gospel, and new involvement in the life of the Church.

85. (3) The development of ecumenical team ministries has already led to the corresponding development of ecumenical training for ordination in interdenominational theological schools. For the ordained staff of such schools, and for their students, similar tensions and educational opportunities arise.

86. For all these reasons ecumenical co-operation between ministers is bound to confront the participating churches with urgent demands that further progress be made towards mutual recognition of different church ministries.

87. All these considerations point to the fact that the mutual recognition of ministries represents much more than doctrinal agreement about them. It involves a readiness throughout the churches to face tensions and conflicts about the minister's role creatively, in a lively dependence upon the Holy Spirit.

V
TOWARDS THE RECOGNITION OF AND THE RECONCILIATION OF MINISTRIES

A. THE UNITY OF THE CHURCH AND THE RECOGNITION OF MINISTRIES

88. For the Church to be one the full mutual recognition of ministries is required. The statement on the unity we seek which was adopted by the New Delhi Assembly (1961) makes this point clearly. As it enumerates the conditions which need to be fulfilled to be able to speak of a fully committed fellowship, it also mentions the ministry. Unity will have been achieved only when members and ministers are recognized throughout the Christian community. It is not only necessary that it be possible for the ministers of one church to be admitted to fulfil certain functions in the other church. This would still be only limited recognition. It must be possible, at least in principle, that ministers be able to fulfil their ministry, upon invitation, in any church. Of course there may be restrictions of an administrative nature which limit the exercise of any ministry to certain areas. Such restrictions can exist within the one Church. But unity requires that the calling to and the fruit of the ministry be recognized everywhere.

89. Division among the churches has often found expression in the mutual rejection of ministries. This rejection is not always due to a difference in the understanding of the ministry as such. Recognition of the minister can be withdrawn because the minister is associated with what is regarded to be error in his community. He cannot be accepted as long as his community persists in its particular confession or ethical decision. As soon as agreement on this point of division has been reached, the minister will also be automatically recognized. Division can also be due, however, to the understanding of the nature of ministry itself and efforts towards unity must, therefore, include the working out of an agreement on the ministry.

90. The sign of the apostolic succession has thus become a major factor of disunity in some cases. It follows that mutual recognition cannot be achieved in the same way between all churches. While

in some conversations the emphasis must be laid on matters of faith which divide, in others attention must centre on the understanding of the ministry itself.

91. A common understanding of the ministry will thus not have the same effect on all relations between the divided churches. This question is certainly of vital importance for all churches, and it is clear that without a common understanding no decisive progress can be made on the road towards unity. But while for some churches a common view and practice of the ministry will not immediately change the situation, for others they would represent the breakthrough which is required. A common understanding is a necessity but it is clear that these efforts need to be supported in each particular case by supplementary approaches towards unity. Full mutual recognition can be achieved only through a multiplicity of individual efforts.

92. Furthermore, the conditions under which divisions occurred must also be taken into account as the achievement of mutual recognition is contemplated. They will determine to a large extent the way to be followed to attain agreement. For instance, mutual recognition between the Roman Catholic Church and the churches of the Reformation can be realized only through a re-examination and re-evaluation of the event of the Reformation at the beginning of the sixteenth century; unity between Anglicans and Methodists must take into account the conditions of their separation in the eighteenth century. This historical dimension should not be over-emphasized, however. Common understanding among all churches is necessary today precisely because the churches have moved beyond the conditions of their separation. A mere re-enacting of the division cannot heal the rift. The churches must move together as they are renewed today.

B. DIFFERENT DEGREES OF RECOGNITION

93. The transition from separation to unity cannot be made all at once. It must be made step by step. The churches find themselves at different stages on the road. While some are very close to mutual agreement, others still find insurmountable obstacles.

In order to understand the present situation it might be useful to distinguish different degrees and modes of mutual recognition.

94. (1) The least degree of mutual recognition—generally achieved among churches participating in the Ecumenical Movement—is that of mutual respect. The minister of the other church is not simply considered as a private individual but as one who is invested with a certain authority, which enables him to be the spokesman for his community. His representative character is recognized, at least for the purpose of carrying out the ecumenical dialogue. This acceptance does not prejudge the spiritual value of his ministry but suspends any negative judgement for the sake of positive encounter. Though no theological conclusions are drawn from this attitude, it has more theological implications than most churches would admit.

95. (2) Another degree of recognition is reached when the ecclesial nature of the other church is acknowledged; then the ministry, though it may not be without defects, cannot be declared to be without any spiritual significance. The ministers are seen to have been raised up by God for the equipping of his people and to be actually engaged in the task assigned to the ordained ministry. Their ministry just lacks the fullness which is promised to the apostolic ministry.

96. While in many cases such recognition does not lead to any practical efforts, it very often provides the basis for extensive collaboration. Though the churches cannot recognize one another as Christ's Church in the full sense of the word, they allow their ministers to work together in many respects. They may engage in common witness in areas of ecumenical experiment or in missionary situations. They may even, where the ecclesiological conditions permit it, preside together over the celebration of the eucharist on exceptional occasions, although their churches have not yet reached a full accord on the eucharist and remain separate from one another.

97. (3) Still another stage is reached when the ministry of the other church is officially acknowledged as the apostolic ministry given by Christ. Such recognition would lead in some cases to full

communion between two churches; in any case it provides the basis for more frequent common celebration of the eucharist.- But for some churches such a development would affect the relations only if agreement on the other divisive issues could be reached as well.

98. (4) The decisive stage is the mutual recognition of the communities, implying the mutual recognition of the ministry. When the churches reach this stage, they agree to recognize the other church as Christ's Church as much as they regard themselves as such. This does not necessarily mean that they need to adopt the same organizational structures but it implies a readiness for interpenetration where demanded by the witness to the gospel.

99. The mutual recognition of the churches and their ministries implied a public act from which point unity would be fully realized. Several forms of such a public act have been proposed: mutual imposition of hands, eucharistic concelebration, solemn worship without a particular rite, the simple reading of a text of union during the course of a celebration. No one liturgical form would be absolutely required, but in any case it would be necessary to proclaim the accomplishment of such mutual recognition publicly. And the common celebration of the Lord's supper would certainly be the place for such a service.

100. This description of stages is obviously schematic. It does not imply that every relation between two churches must pass through all those stages. The procedure in each context will vary according to local situations. This description simply represents an attempt to identify the different degrees of recognition which can actually be found among the churches.

C. PROPOSALS FOR ADVANCING ON THE WAY TOWARDS MUTUAL RECOGNITION

101. In order to advance towards the goal expressed in the New Delhi statement, deliberate efforts are required. Discussion can help to clarify the issues but discussion alone will not solve the problem. The churches must ready themselves for actual changes in their approach and their practice.

102. According to what was said above, two things are of crucial importance for mutual recognition of ordination practice. First, the rite used must express the intention to transmit the apostolic ministry of the word of God and of the sacraments. Second, the rite must include an invocation (*epiclesis*) of the Holy Spirit and the laying-on-of-hands. The invocation of the Holy Spirit is intended to safeguard and to attest what in some traditions is called the 'sacramentality' of ordination.

In order to achieve mutual recognition, different steps are required of different churches:

103. (1) (*a*). Churches which have preserved the episcopal succession have to recognize the real content of the ordained ministry that exists in churches that do not have such an episcopal succession. In spite of the mutual separation of both kinds of church, the God who is ever faithful to his promises gives to the communities that lack the episcopal succession but that live in a succession of apostolic faith, a ministry of the Word and Sacrament, the value of which is attested by its fruits. These communities have also, in many cases, developed a vital lay ministry.

104. (*b*) The churches without episcopal succession have to realize that churches which value such succession have also retained a ministry of word and sacraments through the centuries and while the former may not lack a succession in the apostolic faith, they do not have the fullness of the *sign* of apostolic succession. If full visible unity is to be achieved, the fullness of the sign of apostolic succession ought to be recovered.

105. (2) (*a*) Churches with episcopal succession should reassert the value of episcopal ministry, particularly in its pastoral aspects, and should work in order that others might discover its significance as a personally embodied sign of visible unity.

106. (*b*) These Churches should also consider the desirability of recognizing some ordained ministries that exist apart from an episcopal succession, but which embody a succession of ordained ministers who combine in their ministries the functions of both bishop and presbyter. It may also be possible to recognize some ministries that do not claim a formal episcopal or episcopal-

presbyteral succession, but that in fact exist with the express intention of maintaining a succession in the apostolic faith.

NOTES

1. Cf. Louvain 1971, Faith and Order report on 'The Ordained Ministry' in *Study Reports and Documents*, Geneva 1971, p. 89.
2. *The Fourth World Conference on Faith and Order:* Report from Montreal 1963, London–New York 9164, p. 63
3. Cf. Louvain 1971, p. 81
4. Cf. ibid., p. 82
5. Cf. ibid., p. 88
6. Cf. ibid., pp. 88–9
7. Cf. ibid., p. 93
8. Cf. ibid., pp. 92–3